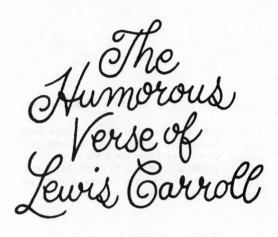

The Humorous Verse of Lewis Carroll

With Illustrations by

SIR JOHN TENNIEL, ARTHUR B. FROST,
HENRY HOLIDAY, HARRY FURNISS,
AND THE AUTHOR

DOVER PUBLICATIONS, INC.
NEW YORK

This new Dover edition, first published in
1960, is an unabridged and unaltered republication of the work first published in 1933
under the title: *The Collected Verse of Lewis
Carroll*. It is published by special arrangement
with the Macmillan Company.

Standard Book Number: 486-20654-8
Library of Congress Catalog Card Number: 60-50681

Manufactured in the United States of America
Dover Publications, Inc.
180 Varick Street
New York, N. Y. 10014

ACKNOWLEDGMENT

The publishers wish to acknowledge with thanks the courteous permissions to use the following material:

To Harvard College Library, which owns the manuscripts of "Puzzles from Wonderland" and "Solutions to Puzzles from Wonderland";

To Mr. Arthur A. Houghton, Jr., who owns the manuscripts of "Maggie's Visit to Oxford" and "Three Sunsets";

To the Century Company for the verses found in "The Life and Letters of Lewis Carroll" by S. Dodgson Collingwood.

PREFACE

THE present volume contains all the verse which appeared in the books by Lewis Carroll published during his lifetime, together with a number of hitherto unpublished juvenile pieces from the original MSS. of *Useful and Instructive Poetry* and *The Rectory Magazine*, in addition to many others collected from Collingwood's *Lewis Carroll Picture-Book* and *Life and Letters of Lewis Carroll*, and from other works now out of print or not readily accessible.

The order followed is mainly chronological, though the serious verses which formed part of the first edition of *Phantasmagoria* (1869) are here given as belonging more appropriately to *Three Sunsets*, in which they were reissued in 1898. The title of *Rhyme? and Reason?* does not appear, since the contents of that volume are included in *Phantasmagoria* and *The Hunting of the Snark*. The Oxford verses are for convenience grouped with *Notes by an Oxford Chiel* (1874). A few of Arthur B. Frost's illustrations to *Phantasmagoria* have been omitted.

The notes in small type at the head of some of the verses have been inserted for the purposes of this edition. The remainder are the author's own.

For the original suggestion which led to the publication of the *Collected Verse*, the publishers are indebted to Mr. J. Boulter, and in the course of its compilation they have received generous help from many

Preface

quarters—in particular from Major C. H. W. Dodgson, representing the Dodgson family, and from Mr. Sidney Herbert Williams, joint author with Mr. Falconer Madan of the invaluable *Handbook of the Literature of the Rev. C. L. Dodgson (Lewis Carroll)*, who allowed " Puzzle " and " Three Children " to be reprinted from his *Some Rare Carrolliana*. They have also to thank the following ladies for assenting to the use of the items with which their names are associated : Miss E. M. Argles ; Mrs. Daniel and Mrs. Lee ; Miss F. M. Forshall ; Mrs. R. G. Hargreaves (*née* Alice Pleasance Liddell) ; Miss Beatrice Hatch ; Mrs. Morton (Miss Margaret Bowman) ; and Mrs. Wyper (Miss Emmie Drury). In addition they have to acknowledge the ready courtesy of the following owners of manuscript verses by Lewis Carroll : Sir Leicester Harmsworth, for "Two Thieves" and the "Prologue to 'La Guida di Bragia'" ; Mr. Arthur A. Houghton, Jr., of New York, for " Maggie's Visit to Oxford " and "Maggie B——" ; Mr. H. F. B. Sharp, for the two poems addressed to Miss Marion Terry ; and of Mr. F. B. de Sausmarez for the text of the second " Prologue." The words of " Dreamland " are reproduced by permission of the Oxford University Press, the publishers of the musical setting by C. E. Hutchinson. Reference must be made in conclusion to the information and assistance freely afforded by Messrs. J. & E. Bumpus, Ltd., Messrs. Maggs Bros., Messrs. Parker & Son, Ltd., of Oxford, Messrs. Sotheby, and Messrs. Henry Sotheran, Ltd.

CONTENTS

Contents

Contents

Contents

THE HUNTING OF THE SNARK

ACROSTICS, INSCRIPTIONS, AND OTHER VERSES

Contents

Contents

EARLY VERSE

EARLY VERSE

MY FAIRY

(From *Useful and Instructive Poetry*, 1845)

I HAVE a fairy by my side
　　Which says I must not sleep,
When once in pain I loudly cried
　　It said "You must not weep."

If, full of mirth, I smile and grin,
　　It says "You must not laugh;"
When once I wished to drink some gin
　　It said "You must not quaff."

When once a meal I wished to taste
　　It said "You must not bite;"
When to the wars I went in haste
　　It said "You must not fight."

"What may I do?" at length I cried,
　　Tired of the painful task.
The fairy quietly replied,
　　And said "You must not ask."

　　Moral: "You mustn't."

3

PUNCTUALITY

(From *Useful and Instructive Poetry*)

MAN naturally loves delay,
   And to procrastinate;
Business put off from day to day
   Is always done too late.

Let every hour be in its place
   Firm fixed, nor loosely shift,
And well enjoy the vacant space,
   As though a birthday gift.

And when the hour arrives, be *there*,
   Where'er that "there" may be;
Uncleanly hands or ruffled hair
   Let no one ever see.

If dinner at "half-past" be placed,
   At "half-past" then be dressed.
If at a "quarter-past" make haste
   To be down with the rest.

Better to be before your time,
   Than e'er to be behind;
To ope the door while strikes the chime,
   That shows a punctual mind.

Punctuality

Moral

Let punctuality and care
    Seize every flitting hour,
So shalt thou cull a floweret fair,
    E'en from a fading flower.

MELODIES

(From *Useful and Instructive Poetry*)

I

THERE was an old farmer of Readall,
Who made holes in his face with a needle,
    They went *far* deeper in
    Than to pierce through the skin,
And yet strange to say he was made beadle.

II

There was an eccentric old draper,
Who wore a hat made of brown paper,
    It went up to a point,
    Yet it looked out of joint,
The cause of which *he* said was "vapour."

III

There was once a young man of Oporta,
Who daily got shorter and shorter,
    The reason he said
    Was the hod on his head,
Which was filled with the *heaviest* mortar.

His sister, named Lucy O'Finner,
Grew constantly thinner and thinner;
    The reason was plain,
    She slept out in the rain,
And was never allowed any dinner.

6

BROTHER AND SISTER

(From *Useful and Instructive Poetry*)

"Sister, sister, go to bed!
Go and rest your weary head."
Thus the prudent brother said.

"Do you want a battered hide,
Or scratches to your face applied?"
Thus his sister calm replied.

"Sister, do not raise my wrath.
I'd make you into mutton broth
As easily as kill a moth!"

The sister raised her beaming eye
And looked on him indignantly
And sternly answered, "Only try!"

Off to the cook he quickly ran.
"Dear Cook, please lend a frying-pan
To me as quickly as you can."

"And wherefore should I lend it you?"
"The reason, Cook, is plain to view.
I wish to make an Irish stew."

7

Brother and Sister

"What meat is in that stew to go?"
"My sister'll be the contents!"
"Oh!"
"You'll lend the pan to me, Cook?"
"No!"

Moral: Never stew your sister.

FACTS

(From *Useful and Instructive Poetry*)

WERE I to take an iron gun,
And fire it off towards the sun;
I grant 'twould reach its mark at last,
But not till many years had passed.

But should that bullet change its force,
And to the planets take its course,
'Twould *never* reach the *nearest* star,
Because it is so *very* far.

9

RULES AND REGULATIONS

(From *Useful and Instructive Poetry*)

A SHORT direction
To avoid dejection,
By variations
In occupations,
And prolongation
Of relaxation,
And combinations
Of recreations,
And disputation
On the state of the nation
In adaptation
To your station,
By invitations
To friends and relations,
By evitation
Of amputation,
By permutation
In conversation,
And deep reflection
You'll avoid dejection.

Learn well your grammar,
And never stammer,
Write well and neatly,
And sing most sweetly,

Rules and Regulations

Be enterprising,
Love early rising,
Go walk of six miles,
Have ready quick smiles,
With lightsome laughter,
Soft flowing after.
Drink tea, not coffee;
Never eat toffy.
Eat bread with butter.
Once more, don't stutter.
Don't waste your money,
Abstain from honey.
Shut doors behind you,
(Don't slam them, mind you.)
Drink beer, not porter.
Don't enter the water
Till to swim you are able.
Sit close to the table.
Take care of a candle.
Shut a door by the handle,
Don't push with your shoulder
Until you are older.
Lose not a button.
Refuse cold mutton.
Starve your canaries.
Believe in fairies.
If you are able,
Don't have a stable
With any mangers.
Be rude to strangers.

Moral: Behave.

HORRORS

(From *The Rectory Magazine*, 1850)

METHOUGHT I walked a dismal place
    Dim horrors all around;
The air was thick with many a face,
    And black as night the ground.

I saw a monster come with speed,
    Its face of grimmliest green,
On human beings used to feed,
    Most dreadful to be seen.

I could not speak, I could not fly,
    I fell down in that place,
I saw the monster's horrid eye
    Come leering in my face!

Amidst my scarcely-stifled groans,
    Amidst my moanings deep,
I heard a voice, "Wake! Mr. Jones,
    You're screaming in your sleep!"

MISUNDERSTANDINGS

(From *The Rectory Magazine*)

I<small>F</small> such a thing had been my thought,
I should have told you so before,
But as I didn't, then you ought
To ask for such a thing no more,
For to teach one who has been taught
Is always thought an awful bore.

Now to commence my argument,
I shall premise an observation,
On which the greatest kings have leant
When striving to subdue a nation,
And e'en the wretch who pays no rent
By it can solve a hard equation.

Its truth is such, the force of reason
Can not avail to shake its power,
Yet e'en the sun in summer season
Doth not dispel so mild a shower
As this, and he who sees it, sees on
Beyond it to a sunny bower—
No more, when ignorance is treason,
Let wisdom's brows be cold and sour.

13

AS IT FELL UPON A DAY

(From *The Rectory Magazine*)

As I was sitting on the hearth
(*And O, but a hog is fat!*)
A man came hurrying up the path,
(*And what care I for that?*)

When he came the house unto,
His breath both quick and short he drew.

When he came before the door,
His face grew paler than before.

When he turned the handle round,
The man fell fainting to the ground.

When he crossed the lofty hall,
Once and again I heard him fall.

When he came up to the turret stair,
He shrieked and tore his raven hair.

When he came my chamber in,
(*And O, but a hog is fat!*)
I ran him through with a golden pin,
(*And what care I for that?*)

YE FATTALE CHEYSE

(From *The Rectory Umbrella*. Illustrated
by the author)

YTTE wes a mirke an dreiry cave,
    Weet scroggis [1] owr ytte creepe.
Gurgles withyn ye flowan wave
    Throw channel braid an deep

Never withyn that dreir recesse
    Wes sene ye lyghte of daye,
Quhat bode azont [2] yts mirkinesse [3]
    Nane kend an nane mote saye.

Ye monarche rade owr brake an brae
    An drave ye yellynge packe,
Hiz meany [4] au' richte cadgily [5]
    Are wendynge [6] yn hiz tracke.

Wi' eager iye, wi' yalpe an crye
    Ye hondes yode [7] down ye rocks,
Ahead of au' their companye
    Renneth ye panky [8] foxe.

Ye foxe hes soughte that cave of awe
    Forewearied [9] wi' hiz rin.
Quha nou ys he sae bauld an braw [10]
    To dare to enter yn?

Wi' eager bounde hes ilka honde
    Gane till that caverne dreir,
Fou [11] many a yowl [12] ys [13] hearde arounde,
    Fou [11] many a screech of feir.

15

Ye Fattale Cheyse

Like ane wi' thirstie appetite
    Quha swalloweth orange pulp,
Wes hearde a huggle an a bite,
    A swallow an a gulp.

Ye kynge hes lap frae aff hiz steid,
    Outbrayde [14] hiz trenchant brande;
"Quha on my packe of hondes doth feed,
    Maun deye benead thilke hande."

Sae sed, sae dune: ye stonderes [15] hearde
    Fou many a mickle [16] stroke,
Sowns [17] lyke ye flappynge of a birde,
    A struggle an a choke.

Owte of ye cave scarce fette [18] they ytte,
    Wi pow [19] an push an hau' [20]—
Whereof Y've drawne a littel bytte,
    Bot durst nat draw ytte au.[21]

¹ bushes.   ² beyond.   ³ darkness.   ⁴ company.
⁵ merrily.   ⁶ going journeying.   ⁷ went.   ⁸ cunning.
⁹ much wearied.   ¹⁰ brave.   ¹¹ full.   ¹² howl.
¹³ is.   ¹⁴ drawn   ¹⁵ bystanders.   ¹⁶ heavy.
¹⁷ sounds.   ¹⁸ fetched.   ¹⁹ pull.   ²⁰ haul.   ²¹ all.

LAYS OF SORROW

No. 1

(From *The Rectory Umbrella*)

THE day was wet, the rain fell souse
    Like jars of strawberry jam,[1] a
Sound was heard in the old henhouse,
    A beating of a hammer.
Of stalwart form, and visage warm,
    Two youths were seen within it,
Splitting up an old tree into perches for their poultry
    At a hundred strokes [2] a minute.

The work is done, the hen has taken
Possession of her nest and eggs,
Without a thought of eggs and bacon,[3]
(Or I am very much mistaken :)
        She turns over each shell,
        To be sure that all's well,
        Looks into the straw
        To see there's no flaw,
        Goes once round the house,[4]
        Half afraid of a mouse,
        Then sinks calmly to rest
        On the top of her nest,
    First doubling up each of her legs.

---

[1] *I.e.* the jam without the jars.   Observe the beauty of this rhyme.
[2] At the rate of a stroke and two-thirds in a second.
[3] Unless the hen was a poacher, which is unlikely.
[4] The henhouse.

17

Lays of Sorrow

Time rolled away, and so did every shell,
    "Small by degrees and beautifully less,"
As the sage mother with a powerful spell [1]
    Forced each in turn its contents to express,[2]
    But ah! "imperfect is expression,"
    Some poet said, I don't care who,
    If you want to know you must go elsewhere,
    One fact I can tell, if you're willing to hear,
    He never attended a Parliament Session,
    For I'm certain that if he had ever been there,
    Full quickly would he have changed his ideas,
    With the hissings, the hootings, the groans and
      the cheers.
    And as to his name it is pretty clear
    That it wasn't me and it wasn't you!

And so it fell upon a day,
    (That is, it never rose again)
A chick was found upon the hay,
Its little life had ebbed away.
No longer frolicsome and gay,
No longer could it run or play.
"And must we, chicken, must we part?"
Its master [3] cried with bursting heart,
    And voice of agony and pain.
So one, whose ticket's marked "Return," [4]
When to the lonely roadside station
He flies in fear and perturbation,
Thinks of his home—the hissing urn—
Then runs with flying hat and hair,

[1] Beak and claw.   [2] Press out.
[3] Probably one of the two stalwart youths.
[4] The system of return tickets is an excellent one. People are conveyed, on particular days, there and back again for one fare.

Lays of Sorrow

And, entering, finds to his despair
    He's missed the very latest train.[1]

Too long it were to tell of each conjecture
    Of chicken suicide, and poultry victim,
The deadly frown, the stern and dreary lecture,
    The timid guess, "perhaps some needle pricked
        him!"
The din of voice, the words both loud and many,
    The sob, the tear, the sigh that none could
        smother,
Till all agreed "a shilling to a penny
    It killed itself, and we acquit the mother!"
    Scarce was the verdict spoken,
    When that still calm was broken,
A childish form hath burst into the throng;
    With tears and looks of sadness,
    That bring no news of gladness,
But tell too surely something hath gone wrong!
"The sight that I have come upon
    The stoutest heart [2] would sicken,
That nasty hen has been and gone
    And killed another chicken!"

[1] An additional vexation would be that his "Return" ticket would be no use the next day.
[2] Perhaps even the "bursting" heart of its master.

LAYS OF SORROW

No. 2

(From *The Rectory Umbrella*. Illustrated by the author)

FAIR stands the ancient [1] Rectory,
  The Rectory of Croft,
The sun shines bright upon it,
  The breezes whisper soft.

From all the house and garden
  Its inhabitants come forth,
And muster in the road without,
And pace in twos and threes about,
  The children of the North.

Some are waiting in the garden,
  Some are waiting at the door,
And some are following behind,
  And some have gone before.
But wherefore all this mustering?
  Wherefore this vast array?
A gallant feat of horsemanship
  Will be performed to-day.

To eastward and to westward,
  The crowd divides amain,

[1] This Rectory has been supposed to have been built in the time of Edward VI, but recent discoveries clearly assign its origin to a much earlier period. A stone has been found in an island formed by the river Tees on which is inscribed the letter "A," which is justly conjectured to stand for the name of the great King Alfred, in whose reign this house was probably built.

Lays of Sorrow

Two youths are leading on the steed,
  Both tugging at the rein;
And sorely do they labour,
  For the steed [1] is very strong,
And backward moves its stubborn feet,
And backward ever doth retreat,
  And drags its guides along.

        And now the knight hath
            mounted,
          Before the admiring band,
        Hath got the stirrups on his feet,
          The bridle in his hand.
        Yet, oh! beware, sir horseman!
          And tempt thy fate no more,
        For such a steed as thou hast got
          Was never rid before!

The rabbits bow before thee,
  And cower in the straw;
The chickens [2] are submissive,
  And own thy will for law;
Bullfinches and canary
  Thy bidding do obey;
And e'en the tortoise in its shell
Doth never say thee nay.

But thy steed will hear no master,
  Thy steed will bear no stick,

---

[1] The poet entreats pardon for having represented a donkey under this dignified name.

[2] A full account of the history and misfortunes of these interesting creatures may be found in the first "Lay of Sorrow."

21

Lays of Sorrow

And woe to those that beat her,
    And woe to those that kick![1]
For though her rider smite her,
    As hard as he can hit,
And strive to turn her from the
    yard,
She stands in silence, pulling
    hard
Against the pulling bit.

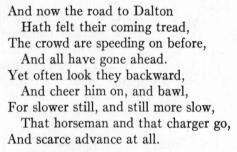

And now the road to Dalton
    Hath felt their coming tread,
The crowd are speeding on before,
    And all have gone ahead.
Yet often look they backward,
    And cheer him on, and bawl,
For slower still, and still more slow,
    That horseman and that charger go,
And scarce advance at all.

And now two roads to choose from
    Are in that rider's sight:
In front the road to Dalton,
    And New Croft upon the
    right.
"I can't get by!" he bellows,
    "I really am not able!
Though I pull my shoulder
    out of joint,
I cannot get him past this
    point,
    For it leads unto his stable!"

[1] It is a singular fact that a donkey makes a point of returning
any kicks offered to it.

Lays of Sorrow

Then out spake Ulfrid Longbow,[1]
  A valiant youth was he,
"Lo! I will stand on thy right hand
  And guard the pass for thee!"

And out spake fair Flureeza,[2]
  His sister eke was she,
"I will abide on thy other side,
  And turn thy steed for thee!"

And now commenced a
    struggle
  Between that steed
    and rider,
For all the strength that
    he hath left
  Doth not suffice to
    guide her.

[1] This valiant knight, besides having a heart of steel and nerves of iron, has been lately in the habit of carrying a brick in his eye.
[2] She was sister to both.

23

Lays of Sorrow

Though Ulfrid and his sister
    Have kindly stopped the way,
And all the crowd have cried aloud,
    "We can't wait here all day!"

Round turned he as not deigning
    Their words to understand,
But he slipped the stirrups from his feet
    The bridle from his hand,
And grasped the mane full lightly,
    And vaulted from his seat,
And gained the road in triumph,[1]
    And stood upon his feet.

All firmly till that moment
    Had Ulfrid Longbow stood,
And faced the foe right valiantly,
    As every warrior should.

[1] The reader will probably be at a loss to discover the nature of this triumph, as no object was gained, and the donkey was obviously the victor; on this point, however, we are sorry to say we can offer no good explanation.

Lays of Sorrow

But when safe on terra firma
  His brother he did spy,
"What *did* you do that for?" he cried,
Then unconcerned he stepped aside
  And let it canter by.

They gave him bread and butter,[1]
  That was of public right,
As much as four strong rabbits
  Could munch from morn to night,
For he'd done a deed of daring,
  And faced that savage steed,
And therefore cups of coffee sweet,
And everything that was a treat,
  Were but his right and meed.

[1] Much more acceptable to a true knight than "corn-land" which the Roman people were so foolish as to give to their daring champion, Horatius.

Lays of Sorrow

And often in the evenings,
  When the fire is blazing
    bright,
When books bestrew the
    table
  And moths obscure the
    light,
When crying children go
    to bed,
  A struggling, kicking
    load;
We'll talk of Ulfrid Long-
    bow's deed,
How, in his brother's ut-
    most need,
Back to his aid he flew
    with speed,
And how he faced the fiery
    steed,
  And kept the New Croft
    Road.

THE TWO BROTHERS

(From *The Rectory Umbrella*, 1853)

THERE were two brothers at Twyford school,
  And when they had left the place,
It was, "Will ye learn Greek and Latin?
  Or will ye run me a race?
Or will ye go up to yonder bridge,
  And there we will angle for dace?"

"I'm too stupid for Greek and for Latin,
  I'm too lazy by half for a race,
So I'll even go up to yonder bridge,
  And there we will angle for dace."

He has fitted together two joints of his rod,
  And to them he has added another,
And then a great hook he took from his book,
  And ran it right into his brother.

Oh much is the noise that is made among boys
  When playfully pelting a pig,
But a far greater pother was made by his brother
  When flung from the top of the brigg.

The fish hurried up by the dozens,
  All ready and eager to bite,
For the lad that he flung was so tender and young,
  It quite gave them an appetite.

27

The Two Brothers

Said he, "Thus shall he wallop about
   And the fish take him quite at their ease,
For me to annoy it was ever his joy,
   Now I'll teach him the meaning of 'Tees'!"

The wind to his ear brought a voice,
   "My brother, you didn't had ought ter!
And what have I done that you think it such fun
   To indulge in the pleasure of slaughter?

"A good nibble or bite is my chiefest delight,
   When I'm merely expected to *see*,
But a bite from a fish is not quite what I wish,
   When I get it performed upon *me;*
And just now here's a swarm of dace at my arm,
   And a perch has got hold of my knee.

"For water my thirst was not great at the first,
   And of fish I have quite sufficien——"
"Oh fear not!" he cried, "for whatever betide,
   We are both in the selfsame condition!

"I am sure that our state's very nearly alike
   (Not considering the question of slaughter),
For I have my perch on the top of the bridge,
   And you have your perch in the water.

"I stick to my perch and your perch sticks to you,
   We are really extremely alike;
I've a turn-pike up here, and I very much fear
   You may soon have a turn with a pike."

"Oh grant but one wish! If I'm took by a fish
   (For your bait is your brother, good man!)

The Two Brothers

Pull him up if you like, but I hope you will strike
 As gently as ever you can."

"If the fish be a trout, I'm afraid there's no doubt
 I must strike him like lightning that's greased;
If the fish be a pike, I'll engage not to strike,
 Till I've waited ten minutes at least."

"But in those ten minutes to desolate Fate
 Your brother a victim may fall!"
"I'll reduce it to five, so *perhaps* you'll survive,
 But the chance is exceedingly small."

"Oh hard is your heart for to act such a part;
 Is it iron, or granite, or steel?"
"Why, I really can't say—it is many a day
 Since my heart was accustomed to feel.

"'Twas my heart-cherished wish for to slay many fish,
 Each day did my malice grow worse,
For my heart didn't soften with doing it so often,
 But rather, I should say, the reverse."

"Oh would I were back at Twyford school,
 Learning lessons in fear of the birch!"
"Nay, brother!" he cried, "for whatever betide,
 You are better off here with your perch!

"I am sure you'll allow you are happier now,
 With nothing to do but to play;
And this single line here, it is perfectly clear,
 Is much better than thirty a day!

"And as to the rod hanging over your head,
 And apparently ready to fall,

The Two Brothers

That, you know, was the case, when you lived in that
place,
So it need not be reckoned at all.

"Do you see that old trout with a turn-up-nose
snout?
(Just to speak on a pleasanter theme,)
Observe, my dear brother, our love for each other—
He's the one I like best in the stream.

"To-morrow I mean to invite him to dine
(We shall all of us think it a treat);
If the day should be fine, I'll just *drop him a line*,
And we'll settle what time we're to meet.

"He hasn't been into society yet,
And his manners are not of the best,
So I think it quite fair that it should be *my* care,
To see that he's properly dressed."

Many words brought the wind of "cruel" and
"kind,"
And that "man suffers more than the brute":
Each several word with patience he heard,
And answered with wisdom to boot.

"What? prettier swimming in the stream,
Than lying all snugly and flat?
Do but look at that dish filled with glittering fish,
Has Nature a picture like that?

"What? a higher delight to be drawn from the sight
Of fish full of life and of glee?
What a noodle you are! 'tis delightfuller far
To kill them than let them go free!

30

The Two Brothers

"I know there are people who prate by the hour
    Of the beauty of earth, sky, and ocean;
Of the birds as they fly, of the fish darting by,
    Rejoicing in Life and in Motion.

"As to any delight to be got from the sight,
    It is all very well for a flat,
But *I* think it all gammon, for hooking a salmon
    Is better than twenty of that!

"They say that a man of a right-thinking mind
    Will *love* the dumb creatures he sees—
What's the use of his mind, if he's never inclined
    To pull a fish out of the Tees?

"Take my friends and my home—as an outcast I'll
      roam:
    Take the money I have in the Bank;
It is just what I wish, but deprive me of *fish*,
    And my life would indeed be a blank!"

Forth from the house his sister came,
    Her brothers for to see,
But when she saw that sight of awe,
    The tear stood in her e'e.

"Oh what bait's that upon your hook,
    My brother, tell to me?"
"It is but the fantailed pigeon,
    He would not sing for me."

"Whoe'er would expect a pigeon to sing,
    A simpleton he must be!
But a pigeon-cote is a different thing
    To the coat that there I see!"

31

The Two Brothers

"Oh what bait's that upon your hook,
  Dear brother, tell to me?"
"It is my younger brother," he cried,
  "Oh woe and dole is me!

"I's mighty wicked, that I is!
  Or how could such things be?
Farewell, farewell, sweet sister,
  I'm going o'er the sea."

"And when will you come back again,
  My brother, tell to me?"
"When chub is good for human food,
  And that will never be!"

She turned herself right round about,
  And her heart brake into three,
Said, "One of the two will be wet through and
    through,
  And t'other'll be late for his tea!"

THE LADY OF THE LADLE

(Published in the *Whitby Gazette*, 1854)

THE Youth at Eve had drunk his fill,
Where stands the "Royal" on the Hill,
And long his mid-day stroll had made,
On the so-called "Marine Parade"—
(Meant, I presume, for Seamen brave,
Whose "march is on the Mountain wave";
'Twere just the bathing-place for him
Who stays on land till he can swim—)
And he had strayed into the Town,
And paced each alley up and down,
Where still, so narrow grew the way,
The very houses seemed to say,
Nodding to friends across the Street,
"One struggle more and we shall meet."
And he had scaled that wondrous stair
That soars from earth to upper air,
Where rich and poor alike must climb,
And walk the treadmill for a time.
That morning he had dressed with care,
And put Pomatum on his hair;
He was, the loungers all agreed,
A very heavy swell indeed:
Men thought him, as he swaggered by,
Some scion of nobility,

33

The Lady of the Ladle

And never dreamed, so cold his look,
That he had loved—and loved a Cook.
Upon the beach he stood and sighed
Unheedful of the treacherous tide;
Thus sang he to the listening main,
And soothed his sorrow with the strain!

CORONACH

"SHE is gone by the Hilda,
　　She is lost unto Whitby,
And her name is Matilda,
　　Which my heart it was smit by;
Tho' I take the Goliah,
　　I learn to my sorrow
That 'it won't,' said the crier,
　　'Be off till to-morrow.'

"She called me her 'Neddy,'
　　(Tho' there mayn't be much in it,)
And I should have been ready,
　　If she'd waited a minute;
I was following behind her
　　When, if you recollect, I
Merely ran back to find a
　　Gold pin for my neck-tie.

"Rich dresser of suet!
　　Prime hand at a sausage!
I have lost thee, I rue it,
　　And my fare for the passage!
Perhaps *she* thinks it funny,
　　Aboard of the Hilda,

34

Coronach

But I've lost purse and money,
    And thee, oh, my 'Tilda!"

His pin of gold the youth undid
And in his waistcoat-pocket hid,
Then gently folded hand in hand,
And dropped asleep upon the sand.

SHE'S ALL MY FANCY PAINTED HIM

(From *Misch-Masch*. An earlier version of the lines read in evidence at the trial of the Knave of Hearts. See p. 69)

[This affecting fragment was found in MS. among the papers of the well-known author of "Was it You or I?" a tragedy, and the two popular novels, "Sister and Son," and "The Niece's Legacy, or the Grateful Grandfather."]

She's all my fancy painted him
    (I make no idle boast);
If he or you had lost a limb,
    Which would have suffered most?

He said that you had been to her,
    And seen me here before;
But, in another character,
    She was the same of yore.

There was not one that spoke to us,
    Of all that thronged the street:
So he sadly got into a 'bus,
    And pattered with his feet.

They sent him word I had not gone
    (We know it to be true);
If she should push the matter on,
    What would become of you?

She's all My Fancy Painted Him

They gave her one, they gave me two,
   They gave us three or more;
They all returned from him to you,
   Though they were mine before.

If I or she should chance to be
   Involved in this affair,
He trusts to you to set them free,
   Exactly as we were.

It seemed to me that you had been
   (Before she had this fit)
An obstacle, that came between
   Him, and ourselves, and it.

Don't let him know she liked them best,
   For this must ever be
A secret, kept from all the rest,
   Between yourself and me.

PHOTOGRAPHY EXTRAORDINARY

(From *Misch-Masch*. Specimens of the results obtained by photographing the mental operations of a young man and developing them to various degrees of intensity representing different Schools of Novels)

The Milk-and-Water School

ALAS! she would not hear my prayer!
Yet it were rash to tear my hair;
Disfigured, I should be less fair.

She was unwise, I may say blind;
Once she was lovingly inclined;
Some circumstance has changed her mind.

The Strong-Minded or Matter-of-Fact School

Well! so my offer was no go!
She might do worse, I told her so;
She was a fool to answer "No."

However, things are as they stood;
Nor would I have her if I could,
For there are plenty more as good.

The Spasmodic or German School

Firebrands and daggers! hope hath fled!
To atoms dash the doubly dead!
My brain is fire—my heart is lead!

Her soul is flint, and what am I?
Scorch'd by her fierce, relentless eye,
Nothingness is my destiny!

LAYS OF MYSTERY, IMAGINATION, AND HUMOUR

No. 1

THE PALACE OF HUMBUG

(From *Misch-Masch*)

I DREAMT I dwelt in marble halls,
And each damp thing that creeps and crawls
Went wobble-wobble on the walls.

Faint odours of departed cheese,
Blown on the dank, unwholesome breeze,
Awoke the never-ending sneeze.

Strange pictures decked the arras drear,
Strange characters of woe and fear,
The humbugs of the social sphere.

One showed a vain and noisy prig,
That shouted empty words and big
At him that nodded in a wig.

And one, a dotard grim and gray,
Who wasteth childhood's happy day
In work more profitless than play.

Whose icy breast no pity warms,
Whose little victims sit in swarms,
And slowly sob on lower forms.

39

The Palace of Humbug

And one, a green thyme-honoured Bank,
Where flowers are growing wild and rank,
Like weeds that fringe a poisoned tank.

All birds of evil omen there
Flood with rich Notes the tainted air,
The witless wanderer to snare.

The fatal Notes neglected fall,
No creature heeds the treacherous call,
For all those goodly Strawn Baits Pall.

The wandering phantom broke and fled,
Straightway I saw within my head
A vision of a ghostly bed,

Where lay two worn decrepit men,
The fictions of a lawyer's pen,
Who never more might breathe again.

The serving-man of Richard Roe
Wept, inarticulate with woe :
She wept, that waited on John Doe.

"Oh rouse," I urged, "the waning sense
With tales of tangled evidence,
Of suit, demurrer, and defence."

"Vain," she replied, "such mockeries :
For morbid fancies, such as these,
No suits can suit, no plea can please."

And bending o'er that man of straw,
She cried in grief and sudden awe,
Not inappropriately, "Law !"

The Palace of Humbug

The well-remembered voice he knew,
He smiled, he faintly muttered "Sue!"
(Her very name was legal too.)

The night was fled, the dawn was nigh:
A hurricane went raving by,
And swept the Vision from mine eye.

Vanished that dim and ghostly bed,
(The hangings, tape; the tape was red:)
'Tis o'er, and Doe and Roe are dead!

Oh, yet my spirit inly crawls,
What time it shudderingly recalls
That horrid dream of marble halls!

Oxford, 1855.

THE MOUSE'S TALE

(Early version, from *Alice's Adventures Underground*)

We lived beneath the mat,
   Warm and snug and fat,
      But one woe, and that
         Was the cat!
           To our joys
           a clog, In
           our eyes a
          fog, On our
         hearts a log
        Was the dog!
      When the
     cat's away,
    T h e n
   the mice
   w i l l
   play.
    But, alas!
    one day (So they say)
      Came the dog and
        cat, Hunting
         f o r a
         r a t,
       Crushed
      the mice
    all flat,
   Each
   one
   as
   he
   sat

Underneath the mat, Warm, and snug, and fat—Think of that!

THE MOCK TURTLE'S SONG

(Early version, from *Alice's Adventures Underground*)

BENEATH the waters of the sea
Are lobsters thick as thick can be—
They love to dance with you and me,
My own, my gentle Salmon!

CHORUS

Salmon, come up! Salmon, go down!
Salmon, come twist your tail around!
Of all the fishes of the sea
There's none so good as Salmon!

UPON THE LONELY MOOR

(An early version of the White Knight's Ballad, from
The Train, 1856)

[IT is always interesting to ascertain the sources
from which our great poets obtained their ideas: this
motive has dictated the publication of the following:
painful as its appearance must be to the admirers of
Wordsworth and his poem of. "Resolution and
Independence."]

> I met an aged, aged man
>   Upon the lonely moor:
> I knew I was a gentleman,
>   And he was but a boor.
> So I stopped and roughly questioned him,
>   "Come, tell me how you live!"
> But his words impressed my ear no more
>   Than if it were a sieve.
>
> He said, "I look for soap-bubbles,
>   That lie among the wheat,
> And bake them into mutton-pies,
>   And sell them in the street.
> I sell them unto men," he said,
>   "Who sail on stormy seas;
> And that's the way I get my bread—
>   A trifle, if you please."

44

Upon the Lonely Moor

But I was thinking of a way
    To multiply by ten,
And always, in the answer, get
    The question back again.
I did not hear a word he said,
    But kicked that old man calm,
And said, "Come, tell me how you live!"
    And pinched him in the arm.

His accents mild took up the tale:
    He said, "I go my ways,
And when I find a mountain-rill,
    I set it in a blaze.
And thence they make a stuff they call
    Rowland's Macassar Oil;
But fourpence-halfpenny is all
    They give me for my toil."

But I was thinking of a plan
    To paint one's gaiters green,
So much the colour of the grass
    That they could ne'er be seen.
I gave his ear a sudden box,
    And questioned him again,
And tweaked his grey and reverend locks,
    And put him into pain.

He said, "I hunt for haddocks' eyes
    Among the heather bright,
And work them into waistcoat-buttons
    In the silent night.
And these I do not sell for gold,
    Or coin of silver-mine,

Upon the Lonely Moor

But for a copper-halfpenny,
   And that will purchase nine.

"I sometimes dig for buttered rolls,
   Or set limed twigs for crabs;
I sometimes search the flowery knolls
   For wheels of hansom cabs.
And that's the way" (he gave a wink)
   "I get my living here,
And very gladly will I drink
   Your Honour's health in beer."

I heard him then, for I had just
   Completed my design
To keep the Menai bridge from rust
   By boiling it in wine.
I duly thanked him, ere I went,
   For all his stories queer,
But chiefly for his kind intent
   To drink my health in beer.

And now if e'er by chance I put
   My fingers into glue,
Or madly squeeze a right-hand foot
   Into a left-hand shoe;
Or if a statement I aver
   Of which I am not sure,
I think of that strange wanderer
   Upon the lonely moor.

MISS JONES

(Reduced facsimile of a medley by Lewis Carroll, written out by his sister Margaret)

Miss Jones

For man is a creature weak & impressible, Thinks such a deal of ap-pearance, my dear.

So she waited for her Simon beside the tanyard gate, Re-gardless of the pieman,

who hinted it was late. Waiting for Simon, she coughed in the chilly night, un-til the

Tanner found her, And kindly brought a light old coat to wrap a-round her. She

felt her cold was getting worse, Yet still she fondly whispered "Oh take your time, my

Simon, although I've waited long. I do not fear my Simon dear will fail to come at

last, Al Though I know that long ago the time I named is past. My Simon! my Simon!

Oh, charming man! oh! charming man! Dear Simon Smith, sweet Simon Smith". Oh,

there goes the church-clock, the town-clock, The station-clock, & there go the other clocks,

they all are striking Twelve! Oh Simon, it is getting late, It's very dull to sit & wait

And really I'm in such a state, I hope you'll come at any rate, quite early in the

morning, quite early in the morning: Then with prancing bays & a yellow chaise We'll away to gretna green,

(8) Wait for the waggon.   (10) Lucy Long   (12) Oh charming May'   (14) So early in the morning
(9) Oft in the stilly night.   (11) Reuben Wright.   (13) Oh weal may the keel row   (15) Some love to roam.

48

Miss Jones

For when I am with my Simon Smith - oh, that common name! Oh that vulgar name!
I shall never rest happy till he's changed that name, *but* when he has married me,
maybe he'll love me to that degree, that he'll grant me my prayer & will call himself "Clare"
So she talked all alone, as she sat upon a stone, still hoping he would come and
find her, and she started most unkimmon, when instead of darling "Simmon" t'was a
strange man that stood be-hind her, who civilly observed "Good evening, m'am, I really
am surprised to see that you're out here alone, for you must own from thieves you're
not secure. A watch, I see. Pray lend it me (I hope the gold is pure) And all those
rings, & other things - Don't scream, you know, for long ago The po-liceman off from
his beat has gone. In the kitchen"- "Oh you desperate villain! Oh you treacherous
thief!" And these were the words of her anger & grief "When first to Simon Smith
I gave my hand I never could have thought he would have acted half so mean with this,

(16) I will marry my own love   (18) The girl I left behind me   (20) The Minstrel boy
(17)   (19) The perfect cure   (21) Beautiful Rhine   (22) Rule Britannia.

49

Miss Jones

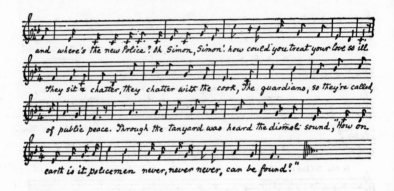

and where's the new Police? Oh Simon, Simon! how could you treat your love so ill

They sit & chatter, they chatter with the cook, The guardians, so they're called,

of public peace. Through the tanyard was heard the dismal sound, "How on

earth is it policemen never, never never, can be found?"

FROM

ALICE'S ADVENTURES IN WONDERLAND

FROM

ALICE'S ADVENTURES IN WONDERLAND

DEDICATION

ALL in the golden afternoon
  Full leisurely we glide;
For both our oars, with little skill,
  By little arms are plied,
While little hands make vain pretence
  Our wanderings to guide.

Ah, cruel Three! In such an hour
  Beneath such dreamy weather,
To beg a tale of breath too weak
  To stir the tiniest feather!
Yet what can one poor voice avail
  Against three tongues together?

Imperious Prima flashes forth
  Her edict "to begin it"—
In gentler tone Secunda hopes
  "There will be nonsense in it!"—
While Tertia interrupts the tale
  Not *more* than once a minute.

53

Dedication

Anon, to sudden silence won,
   In fancy they pursue
The dream-child moving through a land
   Of wonders wild and new,
In friendly chat with bird or beast—
   And half believe it true.

And ever, as the story drained
   The wells of fancy dry,
And faintly strove that weary one
   To put the subject by,
" The rest next time—" " It *is* next time ! "
   The happy voices cry.

Thus grew the tale of Wonderland :
   Thus slowly, one by one,
Its quaint events were hammered out—
   And now the tale is done,
And home we steer, a merry crew,
   Beneath the setting sun.

Alice ! a childish story take,
   And with a gentle hand
Lay it where Childhood's dreams are twined
   In Memory's mystic band,
Like pilgrim's wither'd wreath of flowers
   Pluck'd in a far-off land.

HOW DOTH . . .

How doth the little crocodile
   Improve his shining tail,
And pour the waters of the Nile
   On every golden scale !

How cheerfully he seems to grin,
   How neatly spreads his claws,
And welcomes little fishes in
   With gently smiling jaws !

THE MOUSE'S TALE

THE MOUSE'S TALE

FURY said to a

                mouse, That he
            met in the
        house,
    " Let us
        both go to
        law : *I* will
                prosecute
                    you. Come,
                        I'll take no
                            denial ; We
                            must have a
                    trial : For
            really this
        morning I've
        nothing
    to do."
        Said the
            mouse to the
                    cur, " Such
                            a trial,
                                dear Sir,
                                    With
                            no jury
                        or judge,
                    would be
                wasting
            our
                breath."
                    " I'll be
                        judge, I'll
                            be jury,"
                                Said
                            cunning
                    old Fury :
                " I'll
                try the
                    whole
                        cause,
                            and
                        condemn
                    you
                    to
                    death."

57

FATHER WILLIAM

"You are old, Father William," the young man
    said,
   "And your hair has become very white;
And yet you incessantly stand on your head—
    Do you think, at your age, it is right?"

"In my youth," Father William replied to his son,
   "I feared it might injure the brain;
But, now that I'm perfectly sure I have none,
    Why, I do it again and again."

"You are old," said the youth, "as I mentioned
  before,
  And have grown most uncommonly fat;
Yet you turned a back-somersault in at the door—
  Pray, what is the reason of that?"

"In my youth," said the sage, as he shook his grey
  locks,
  "I kept all my limbs very supple
By the use of this ointment—one shilling the box—
  Allow me to sell you a couple?"

"You are old," said the youth, "and your jaws are
     too weak
     For anything tougher than suet;
Yet you finished the goose, with the bones and the
     beak—
     Pray, how did you manage to do it?"

"In my youth," said his father, "I took to the
     law,
     And argued each case with my wife;
And the muscular strength, which it gave to my
     jaw,
     Has lasted the rest of my life."

"You are old," said the youth, "one would hardly
suppose
    That your eye was as steady as ever;
Yet you balanced an eel on the end of your nose—
    What made you so awfully clever?"

"I have answered three questions, and that is
enough,"
    Said his father; "don't give yourself airs!
Do you think I can listen all day to such stuff?
    Be off, or I'll kick you down stairs!"

THE DUCHESS'S LULLABY

SPEAK roughly to your little boy,
　　And beat him when he sneezes :
He only does it to annoy,
　　Because he knows it teases.

CHORUS.

Wow! wow! wow!

I speak severely to my boy,
　　I beat him when he sneezes ;
For he can thoroughly enjoy
　　The pepper when he pleases !

CHORUS.

Wow! wow! wow!

THE MAD HATTER'S SONG

TWINKLE, twinkle, little bat !
How I wonder what you're at !
Up above the world you fly,
Like a tea-tray in the sky.
                Twinkle, twinkle—

THE MOCK TURTLE'S SONG

"WILL you walk a little faster?" said a whiting to a
   snail.
"There's a porpoise close behind us, and he's treading
   on my tail.
See how eagerly the lobsters and the turtles all advance!
They are waiting on the shingle—will you come and
   join the dance?
   Will you, won't you, will you, won't you, will you
      join the dance?
   Will you, won't you, will you, won't you, won't you
      join the dance?

The Mock Turtle's Song

" You can really have no notion how delightful it will be,
When they take us up and throw us, with the lobsters,
    out to sea ! "
But the snail replied " Too far, too far ! " and gave a
    look askance—
Said he thanked the whiting kindly, but he would not
    join the dance.
    Would not, could not, would not, could not, would
        not join the dance.
    Would not, could not, would not, could not, could
        not join the dance.

" What matters it how far we go ? " his scaly friend
    replied.
" There is another shore, you know, upon the other
    side.
The further off from England the nearer is to France—
Then turn not pale, beloved snail, but come and join
    the dance.
    Will you, won't you, will you, won't you, will you
        join the dance ?
    Will you, won't you, will you, won't you, won't you
        join the dance ? "

ALICE'S RECITATION

'Tis the voice of the Lobster; I heard him declare,
"You have baked me too brown, I must sugar my
    hair."
As a duck with its eyelids, so he with his nose
Trims his belt and his buttons, and turns out his toes.
When the sands are all dry, he is gay as a lark,
And will talk in contemptuous tones of the Shark:
But, when the tide rises and sharks are around,
His voice has a timid and tremulous sound.

Alice's Recitation

I PASSED by his garden, and marked, with one eye,
How the Owl and the Panther were sharing a pie :
The Panther took pie-crust, and gravy, and meat,
While the Owl had the dish as its share of the treat.[1]
When the pie was all finished, the Owl, as a boon,
Was kindly permitted to pocket the spoon :
While the Panther received knife and fork with a
    growl,
And concluded the banquet by——

Later concluded by the author thus :

But the Panther obtained both the fork and the knife,
So, when *he* lost his temper, the Owl lost its life.

[1] In the eight-line version supplied by the author for William
Boyd's musical setting, the second stanza is :—

> I passed by his garden, and marked, with one eye,
> How the owl and the oyster were sharing a pie ;
> While the duck and the Dodo, the lizard and cat
> Were swimming in milk round the brim of a hat.

TURTLE SOUP

Beautiful Soup, so rich and green,
Waiting in a hot tureen !
Who for such dainties would not stoop ?
Soup of the evening, beautiful Soup !
Soup of the evening, beautiful Soup !
    Beau—ootiful Soo—oop !
    Beau—ootiful Soo—oop !
Soo—oop of the e—e—evening,
    Beautiful, beautiful Soup !

Beautiful Soup ! Who cares for fish,
Game, or any other dish ?
Who would not give all else for two p
ennyworth only of beautiful Soup ?
Pennyworth only of beautiful Soup ?
    Beau—ootiful Soo—oop !
    Beau—ootiful Soo—oop !
Soo—oop of the e—e—evening,
    Beautiful, beauti—FUL SOUP !

EVIDENCE READ AT THE TRIAL OF
THE KNAVE OF HEARTS

THEY told me you had been to her,
    And mentioned me to him :
She gave me a good character,
    But said I could not swim.

He sent them word I had not gone,
    (We know it to be true) :
If she should push the matter on,
    What would become of you ?

I gave her one, they gave him two,
    You gave us three or more ;
They all returned from him to you,
    Though they were mine before.

If I or she should chance to be
    Involved in this affair,
He trusts to you to set them free,
    Exactly as we were.

My notion was that you had been
    (Before she had this fit)
An obstacle that came between
    Him, and ourselves, and it.

The Knave of Hearts

Don't let him know she liked them best,
    For this must ever be
A secret kept from all the rest,
    Between yourself and me.

CHRISTMAS GREETINGS

LADY dear, if Fairies may
  For a moment lay aside
Cunning tricks and elfish play,
  'Tis at happy Christmas-tide.

We have heard the children say—
  Gentle children, whom we love—
Long ago, on Christmas-Day,
  Came a message from above.

Still, as Christmas-tide comes round,
  They remember it again—
Echo still the joyful sound,
  " Peace on earth, good-will to men."

Yet the hearts must child-like be
  Where such heavenly guests abide ;
Unto children, in their glee,
  All the year is Christmas-tide.

Thus, forgetting tricks and play
  For a moment, Lady dear,
We would wish you, if we may,
  Merry Christmas, glad New Year !

Christmas, 1867.

PUZZLES FROM WONDERLAND

PUZZLES FROM WONDERLAND

I

DREAMING of apples on a wall,
    And dreaming often, dear,
I dreamed that, if I counted all,
    —How many would appear?

II

A stick I found that weighed two pound:
    I sawed it up one day
In pieces eight of equal weight!
    How much did each piece weigh?
(Everybody says "a quarter of a pound," which is
    wrong.)

III

John gave his brother James a box:
About it there were many locks.

James woke and said it gave him pain;
So gave it back to John again.

The box was not with lid supplied,
Yet caused two lids to open wide:

And all these locks had never a key—
What kind of a box, then, could it be?

75

Puzzles from Wonderland

IV

What is most like a bee in May?
  "Well, let me think: perhaps—" you say.
Bravo! You're guessing well to-day!

V

  Three sisters at breakfast were feeding the cat,
The first gave it sole—Puss was grateful for that:
  The next gave it salmon—which Puss thought a
    treat:
The third gave it herring—which Puss wouldn't eat.
      (Explain the conduct of the cat.)

VI

    Said the Moon to the Sun,
      "Is the daylight begun?"
    Said the Sun to the Moon,
      "Not a minute too soon."

    "You're a Full Moon," said he.
      She replied with a frown,
    "Well! I never *did* see
      So uncivil a clown!"
  (Query. Why was the moon so angry?)

VII

  When the King found that his money was nearly all
gone, and that he really *must* live more economically,
he decided on sending away most of his Wise Men.
There were some hundreds of them—very fine old men,
and magnificently dressed in green velvet gowns with

Puzzles from Wonderland

gold buttons: if they *had* a fault, it was that they always contradicted one another when he asked for their advice—and they certainly ate and drank enormously. So, on the whole, he was rather glad to get rid of them. But there was an old law, which he did not dare to disobey, which said that there must always be

"Seven blind of both eyes:
Two blind of one eye:
Four that see with both eyes:
Nine that see with one eye."
(Query. How many did he keep?)

SOLUTIONS TO PUZZLES FROM WONDERLAND

I

Ten.

II

In Shylock's bargain for the flesh was found
No mention of the blood that flowed around:
So when the stick was sawed in eight,
The sawdust lost diminished from the weight.

III

As curly-headed Jemmy was sleeping in bed,
His brother John gave him a blow on the head;
James opened his eyelids, and spying his brother,
Doubled his fist, and gave him another.

Solutions to Puzzles from Wonderland

This kind of box then is not so rare;
The lids are the eyelids, the locks are the hair,
And so every schoolboy can tell to his cost,
The key to the tangles is constantly lost.

IV

'Twixt "Perhaps" and "May be"
Little difference we see:
Let the question go round,
The answer is found.

V

That salmon and sole Puss should think very grand
Is no such remarkable thing.
For more of these dainties Puss took up her stand;
But when the third sister stretched out her fair hand
Pray why should Puss swallow her ring?

VI

"In these degenerate days," we oft hear said,
"Manners are lost and chivalry is dead!"
No wonder, since in high exalted spheres
The same degeneracy, in fact, appears.
The Moon, in social matters interfering,
Scolded the Sun, when early in appearing;
And the rude Sun, her gentle sex ignoring,
Called her a fool, thus her pretensions flooring.

VII

Five seeing, and seven blind
Give us twelve, in all, we find;

Solutions to Puzzles from Wonderland

But all of these, 'tis very plain,
  Come into account again.
For take notice, it may be true,
  That those blind of one eye are blind for two;
And consider contrariwise,
  That to see with your eye you may have your eyes;
So setting one against the other—
  For a mathematician no great bother—
And working the sum, you will understand
  That sixteen wise men still trouble the land.

FROM

THROUGH THE LOOKING–GLASS

FROM

THROUGH THE LOOKING-GLASS

DEDICATION

CHILD of the pure unclouded brow
  And dreaming eyes of wonder !
Though time be fleet, and I and thou
  Are half a life asunder,
Thy loving smile will surely hail
The love-gift of a fairy-tale.

I have not seen thy sunny face,
  Nor heard thy silver laughter ;
No thought of me shall find a place
  In thy young life's hereafter—
Enough that now thou wilt not fail
To listen to my fairy-tale.

A tale begun in other days,
  When summer suns were glowing—
A simple chime, that served to time
  The rhythm of our rowing—
Whose echoes live in memory yet,
Though envious years would say " forget."

Dedication

Come, hearken then, ere voice of dread,
  With bitter tidings laden,
Shall summon to unwelcome bed
  A melancholy maiden !
We are but older children, dear,
Who fret to find our bedtime near.

Without, the frost, the blinding snow,
  The storm-wind's moody madness—
Within, the firelight's ruddy glow
  And childhood's nest of gladness.
The magic words shall hold thee fast :
Thou shalt not heed the raving blast.

And though the shadow of a sigh
  May tremble through the story,
For " happy summer days " gone by,
  And vanish'd summer glory—
It shall not touch with breath of bale
The pleasance of our fairy-tale.

JABBERWOCKY [1]

'TWAS brillig, and the slithy toves
    Did gyre and gimble in the wabe;
All mimsy were the borogoves,
    And the mome raths outgrabe.

[1] See page 268.

Jabberwocky

" Beware the Jabberwock, my son !
　　The jaws that bite, the claws that catch !
Beware the Jubjub bird, and shun
　　The frumious Bandersnatch ! "

He took his vorpal sword in hand :
　　Long time the manxome foe he sought—
So rested he by the Tumtum tree,
　　And stood awhile in thought.

And as in uffish thought he stood,
　　The Jabberwock, with eyes of flame,
Came whiffling through the tulgey wood,
　　And burbled as it came !

One, two ! One, two ! And through and
　　　　through
The vorpal blade went snicker-snack !
He left it dead, and with its head
　　He went galumphing back.

" And hast thou slain the Jabberwock ?
　　Come to my arms, my beamish boy !
O frabjous day ! Callooh ! Callay ! "
　　He chortled in his joy.

'Twas brillig, and the slithy toves
　　Did gyre and gimble in the wabe ;
All mimsy were the borogoves,
　　And the mome raths outgrabe.

THE JABBERWOCK, WITH EYES OF FLAME

THE WALRUS AND THE CARPENTER

THE sun was shining on the sea,
    Shining with all his might :
He did his very best to make
    The billows smooth and bright—
And this was odd, because it was
    The middle of the night.

The moon was shining sulkily,
    Because she thought the sun
Had got no business to be there
    After the day was done—
" It's very rude of him," she said,
    " To come and spoil the fun ! "

The sea was wet as wet could be,
    The sands were dry as dry.

The Walrus and the Carpenter

You could not see a cloud, because
  No cloud was in the sky :
No birds were flying overhead—
  There were no birds to fly.

The Walrus and the Carpenter
  Were walking close at hand ;
They wept like anything to see
  Such quantities of sand :
" If this were only cleared away,"
  They said, " it *would* be grand ! "

" If seven maids with seven mops
  Swept it for half a year,
Do you suppose," the Walrus said,
  " That they could get it clear ? "
" I doubt it," said the Carpenter,
  And shed a bitter tear.

" O Oysters, come and walk with us ! "
  The Walrus did beseech.
" A pleasant walk, a pleasant talk,
  Along the briny beach :
We cannot do with more than four,
  To give a hand to each."

The eldest Oyster looked at him,
  But never a word he said :
The eldest Oyster winked his eye,
  And shook his heavy head—
Meaning to say he did not choose
  To leave the oyster-bed.

The Walrus and the Carpenter

But four young Oysters hurried up,
 All eager for the treat :
Their coats were brushed, their faces washed,
 Their shoes were clean and neat—
And this was odd, because, you know,
 They hadn't any feet.

Four other Oysters followed them,
 And yet another four ;
And thick and fast they came at last,
 And more, and more, and more—
All hopping through the frothy waves,
 And scrambling to the shore.

The Walrus and the Carpenter
 Walked on a mile or so,
And then they rested on a rock
 Conveniently low :

The Walrus and the Carpenter

And all the little Oysters stood
　　And waited in a row.

" The time has come," the Walrus said,
　　" To talk of many things :
Of shoes—and ships—and sealing-wax—
　　Of cabbages—and kings—
And why the sea is boiling hot—
　　And whether pigs have wings."

" But wait a bit," the Oysters cried,
　　" Before we have our chat ;
For some of us are out of breath,
　　And all of us are fat ! "
" No hurry ! " said the Carpenter.
　　They thanked him much for that.

" A loaf of bread," the Walrus said,
　　" Is what we chiefly need :
Pepper and vinegar besides
　　Are very good indeed—
Now if you're ready, Oysters dear,
　　We can begin to feed."

" But not on us ! " the Oysters cried,
　　Turning a little blue.
" After such kindness, that would be
　　A dismal thing to do ! "
" The night is fine," the Walrus said.
　　" Do you admire the view ?

" It was so kind of you to come !
　　And you are very nice ! "

The Walrus and the Carpenter

The Carpenter said nothing but
    " Cut us another slice :
I wish you were not quite so deaf—
    I've had to ask you twice ! "

" It seems a shame," the Walrus said,
    " To play them such a trick,
After we've brought them out so far,
    And made them trot so quick ! "
The Carpenter said nothing but
    " The butter's spread too thick ! "

" I weep for you," the Walrus said :
    " I deeply sympathize."
With sobs and tears he sorted out
    Those of the largest size,
Holding his pocket-handkerchief
    Before his streaming eyes.

The Walrus and the Carpenter

" O Oysters," said the Carpenter,
" You've had a pleasant run !
Shall we be trotting home again ? "
　　But answer came there none—
And this was scarcely odd, because
　　They'd eaten every one.

HUMPTY DUMPTY'S RECITATION

In winter, when the fields are white,
I sing this song for your delight——

In spring, when woods are getting green,
I'll try and tell you what I mean.

In summer, when the days are long,
Perhaps you'll understand the song :

In autumn, when the leaves are brown,
Take pen and ink, and write it down.

I sent a message to the fish :
I told them " This is what I wish."

The little fishes of the sea,
They sent an answer back to me.

The little fishes' answer was
" We cannot do it, Sir, because——"

I sent to them again to say
" It will be better to obey."

The fishes answered with a grin,
" Why, what a temper you are in ! "

I told them once, I told them twice :
They would not listen to advice.

94

Humpty Dumpty's Recitation

I took a kettle large and new,
Fit for the deed I had to do.

My heart went hop, my heart went thump;
I filled the kettle at the pump.

Then someone came to me and said
" The little fishes are in bed."

I said to him, I said it plain,
" Then you must wake them up again."

I said it very loud and clear;
I went and shouted in his ear.

Humpty Dumpty's Recitation

But he was very stiff and proud ;
He said " You needn't shout so loud ! "

And he was very proud and stiff ;
He said " I'd go and wake them, if——"

I took a corkscrew from the shelf :
I went to wake them up myself.

And when I found the door was locked,
I pulled and pushed and kicked and knocked.

And when I found the door was shut,
I tried to turn the handle, but——

THE WHITE KNIGHT'S BALLAD

I'LL tell thee everything I can;
   There's little to relate.
I saw an aged aged man,
   A-sitting on a gate.
" Who are you, aged man ? " I said.
   " And how is it you live ? "
And his answer trickled through my head
   Like water through a sieve.

He said " I look for butterflies
   That sleep among the wheat :
I make them into mutton-pies,
   And sell them in the street.
I sell them unto men," he said,
   " Who sail on stormy seas ;
And that's the way I get my bread—
   A trifle, if you please."

The White Knight's Ballad

But I was thinking of a plan
  To dye one's whiskers green,
And always use so large a fan
  That they could not be seen.
So, having no reply to give
  To what the old man said,
I cried " Come, tell me how you live ! "
  And thumped him on the head.

His accents mild took up the tale :
  He said " I go my ways,
And when I find a mountain-rill,
  I set it in a blaze ;
And thence they make a stuff they call
  Rowland's Macassar Oil—
Yet twopence-halfpenny is all
  They give me for my toil."

But I was thinking of a way
  To feed oneself on batter,
And so go on from day to day
  Getting a little fatter.
I shook him well from side to side,
  Until his face was blue :
" Come, tell me how you live," I cried
  " And what it is you do ! "

He said " I hunt for haddocks' eyes
  Among the heather bright,
And work them into waistcoat-buttons
  In the silent night.
And these I do not sell for gold
  Or coin of silvery shine,

The White Knight's Ballad

But for a copper halfpenny,
    And that will purchase nine.

"I sometimes dig for buttered rolls,
    Or set limed twigs for crabs;
I sometimes search the grassy knolls
    For wheels of hansom-cabs.
And that's the way" (he gave a wink)
    "By which I get my wealth—
And very gladly will I drink
    Your Honour's noble health."

I heard him then, for I had just
    Completed my design
To keep the Menai bridge from rust
    By boiling it in wine.
I thanked him much for telling me
    The way he got his wealth,
But chiefly for his wish that he
    Might drink my noble health.

And now, if e'er by chance I put
    My fingers into glue,
Or madly squeeze a right-hand foot
    Into a left-hand shoe,
Or if I drop upon my toe
    A very heavy weight,
I weep, for it reminds me so
Of that old man I used to know—
Whose look was mild, whose speech was slow,
Whose hair was whiter than the snow,
Whose face was very like a crow,
With eyes, like cinders, all aglow,

The White Knight's Ballad

Who seemed distracted with his woe,
Who rocked his body to and fro,
And muttered mumblingly and low,
As if his mouth were full of dough,
Who snorted like a buffalo—
That summer evening long ago
   A-sitting on a gate.

THE RED QUEEN'S LULLABY

HUSH-A-BY lady, in Alice's lap !
Till the feast's ready, we've time for a nap :
When the feast's over, we'll go to the ball—
Red Queen, and White Queen, and Alice, and all !

WELCOME QUEEN ALICE

To the Looking-Glass world it was Alice that said
" I've a sceptre in hand, I've a crown on my head;
Let the Looking-Glass creatures, whatever they be,
Come and dine with the Red Queen, the White Queen,
      and me ! "

Then fill up the glasses as quick as you can,
And sprinkle the table with buttons and bran .
Put cats in the coffee, and mice in the tea—
And welcome Queen Alice with thirty-times-three !

" O Looking-Glass creatures," quoth Alice, " draw
      near !
'Tis an honour to see me, a favour to hear :
'Tis a privilege high to have dinner and tea
Along with the Red Queen, the White Queen, and
      me ! "

Then fill up the glasses with treacle and ink,
Or anything else that is pleasant to drink ;
Mix sand with the cider, and wool with the wine—
And welcome Queen Alice with ninety-times-nine !

THE WHITE QUEEN'S RIDDLE

" First the fish must be caught."
That is easy : a baby, I think, could have caught it.
    " Next, the fish must be bought."
That is easy : a penny, I think, would have bought it.

    " Now cook me the fish ! "
That is easy, and will not take more than a minute.
    " Let it lie in a dish ! "
That is easy, because it already is in it.

    " Bring it here ! Let me sup ! "
It is easy to set such a dish on the table.
    " Take the dish-cover up ! "
Ah, *that* is so hard that I fear I'm unable !

    For it holds it like glue——
Holds the lid to the dish, while it lies in the middle :
    Which is easiest to do,
Un-dish-cover the fish, or dishcover the riddle ?

[*The answer is :* an Oyster.]

(Acrostic)

A BOAT, beneath a sunny sky,
Lingering onward dreamily
In an evening of July—

Children three that nestle near,
Eager eye and willing ear,
Pleased a simple tale to hear—

Long has paled that sunny sky:
Echoes fade and memories die:
Autumn frosts have slain July.

Still she haunts me, phantomwise,
Alice moving under skies
Never seen by waking eyes.

Children yet, the tale to hear,
Eager eye and willing ear,
Lovingly shall nestle near.

In a Wonderland they lie,
Dreaming as the days go by,
Dreaming as the summers die:

Ever drifting down the stream—
Lingering in the golden gleam—
Life, what is it but a dream?

PROLOGUES TO PLAYS

PROLOGUE TO "LA GUIDA DI BRAGIA"

(From a Ballad Opera, a skit on Bradshaw's Railway Guide,
for the author's Marionette Theatre)

SHALL soldiers tread the murderous path of war,
Without a notion what they do it for?
Shall pallid mercers drive a roaring trade,
And sell the stuffs their hands have never made?
And shall not we, in this our mimic scene,
Be all that better actors e'er have been?
Awake again a Kemble's tragic tone,
And make a Liston's humour all our own?
Or vie with Mrs. Siddons in the art
To rouse the feelings and to charm the heart?
While Shakespeare's self, with all his ancient fires,
Lights up the forms that tremble on our wires?
Why can't we have, in theatres ideal,
The good, without the evil of the real?
Why may not Marionettes be just as good
As larger actors made of flesh and blood?
Presumptuous thought! to you and your applause
In humbler confidence we trust our cause.

PROLOGUE

(For an amateur performance of two plays at the house of Dr.
Edwin Hatch, Vice-principal of St. Mary Hall, the father of two of
the author's girl-friends, the Misses Beatrice and Ethel Hatch)

*Curtain rises and discovers the Speaker, who comes
forward, thinking aloud,*

"Ladies and Gentlemen" seems stiff and cold.
There's something personal in "Young and Old";
I'll try "Dear Friends" (*addresses audience*)
                              Oh! let me call you so.
Dear friends, look kindly on our little show.
Contrast us not with giants in the Art,
Nor say "You should see Sothern in that part";
Nor yet, unkindest cut of all, in fact,
Condemn the actors, while you praise the Act.
Having by coming proved you find a charm in it,
Don't go away, and hint there may be harm in it.

            .   .   .   .

Miss Crabb.   My dear Miss Verjuice, can it really be?
You're just in time, love, for a cup of tea;
And so, you went to see those people play.
Miss Verjuice.   Well! yes, Miss Crabb, and I may
            truly say
You showed your wisdom when you stayed *away*.
Miss C.   Doubtless!   Theatricals in *our* quiet town!
I've always said, "The law should put them down,"

They mean no harm, tho' I begin to doubt it—
But now sit down and tell me all about it.
Miss V. Well then, Miss Crabb, I won't deceive
    you, dear;
    I heard some things I——didn't like to hear:
Miss C. But don't omit them now.
Miss V.   Well! No! I'll try
    To tell you *all* the painful history.

    (*They whisper alternately behind a small fan.*)

Miss V. And then, my dear, Miss Asterisk and he
    Pretended they were lovers!!
Miss C.   Gracious me!!

    (*More whispering behind fan.*)

        .   .   .   .

Speaker.
    What! *Acting* love!! And has that ne'er been
        seen
    Save with a row of footlights placed between?
    My gentle censors, let me roundly ask,
    Do none but actors ever wear a mask?
    Or have we reached at last that golden age
    That finds deception only on the Stage?
    Come, let's confess all round before we budge,
    When all are guilty, none should play the Judge.
    We're actors all, a motley company,
    Some on the Stage, and others—on the sly—
    And guiltiest he who paints so well his phiz
    His brother actors scarce know what he is.
    A truce to moralizing; we invite
    The goodly company we see to-night
    To have the little banquet we have got,
    Well dressed, we hope, and served up *hot & hot.*

Prologues to Plays

"Loan of a Lover" is the leading dish,
Concluding with a dainty course of fish;
"Whitebait at Greenwich" in the best condition
(By Mr. Gladstone's very kind permission).
Before the courses will be handed round
An *Entrée* made of Children, nicely browned.
                                            Bell rings.
But hark! The bell to summon me away;
They're anxious to begin their little Play.
One word before I go—We'll do our best,
And crave your kind indulgence for the rest;
Own that at least we've striven to succeed,
And take the good intention for the deed.

    Nov. 1871.

PROLOGUE

(Written for an amateur performance at Dr. Hatch's house)

Enter Beatrice, leading Wilfrid. She leaves him at centre (front), and after going round on tip-toe, to make sure they are not overheard, returns and takes his arm.

B. "Wiffie! I'm *sure* that something *is* the matter,
All day there's been—oh, *such* a fuss and clatter!
Mama's been trying on a funny dress—
I never *saw* the house in such a mess!

> (*puts her arm round his neck*)

Is there a secret, Wiffie?"

> W. (*shaking her off*) "Yes, of course!"

B. "And you won't tell it? (*whimpers*) Then you're
very cross!

> (*turns away from him and clasps her hands, looking up ecstatically*)

I'm sure of *this!* It's something *quite* uncommon!"

W. (*stretching up his arms, with a mock-heroic air*)
"Oh, Curiosity! Thy name is Woman!

> (*puts his arm round her coaxingly*)

Well, Birdie, then I'll tell! (*mysteriously*) What
should you say
If they were going to act—a little play?"

III

Prologues to Plays

B. (*jumping and clapping her hands*)
    "I'd say 'HOW NICE!'"
        W. (*pointing to audience*)
          "But will it please the rest?"

B. "Oh *yes!* Because, you know, they'll do their best!

    (*turns to audience*)

You'll praise them, won't you, when you've seen the play?

Just say 'HOW NICE!' before you go away!"

    (*They run away hand in hand.*)

Feb. 14, 1873.

PHANTASMAGORIA

PHANTASMAGORIA

Canto I

The Trystyng

ONE winter night, at half-past nine,
      Cold, tired, and cross, and muddy,
I had come home, too late to dine,
And supper, with cigars and wine,
      Was waiting in the study.

There was a strangeness in the room,
      And Something white and wavy
Was standing near me in the gloom—
I took it for the carpet-broom
      Left by that careless slavey.

But presently the Thing began
      To shiver and to sneeze :
On which I said " Come, come, my man !
That 's a most inconsiderate plan.
      Less noise there, if you please ! "

" I 've caught a cold," the Thing replies,
      " Out there upon the landing."
I turned to look in some surprise,
And there, before my very eyes,
      A little Ghost was standing !

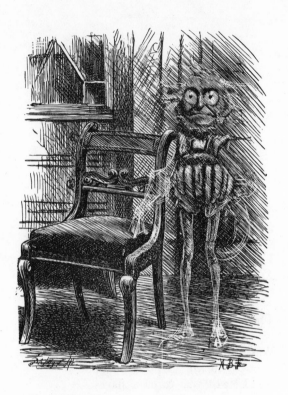

He trembled when he caught my eye,
    And got behind a chair.
"How came you here," I said, "and why?
I never saw a thing so shy.
    Come out! Don't shiver there!"

He said "I'd gladly tell you how,
    And also tell you why;
But" (here he gave a little bow)
"You're in so bad a temper now,
    You'd think it all a lie.

116

The Trystyng

" And as to being in a fright,
    Allow me to remark
That Ghosts have just as good a right,
In every way, to fear the light,
    As Men to fear the dark."

" No plea," said I, " can well excuse
    Such cowardice in you :
For Ghosts can visit when they choose,
Whereas we Humans can't refuse
    To grant the interview."

He said " A flutter of alarm
    Is not unnatural, is it ?
I really feared you meant some harm :
But, now I see that you are calm,
    Let me explain my visit.

" Houses are classed, I beg to state,
    According to the number
Of Ghosts that they accommodate :
(The Tenant merely counts as *weight*,
    With Coals and other lumber).

" This is a ' one-ghost ' house, and you,
    When you arrived last summer,
May have remarked a Spectre who
Was doing all that Ghosts can do
    To welcome the new-comer.

" In Villas this is always done—
    However cheaply rented :
For, though of course there 's less of fun
When there is only room for one,
    Ghosts have to be contented.

117

The Trystyng

" That Spectre left you on the Third—
    Since then you 've not been haunted :
For, as he never sent us word,
'Twas quite by accident we heard
    That any one was wanted.

" A Spectre has first choice, by right,
    In filling up a vacancy ;
Then Phantom, Goblin, Elf, and Sprite—
If all these fail them, they invite
    The nicest Ghoul that they can see.

" The Spectres said the place was low,
    And that you kept bad wine :
So, as a Phantom had to go,
And I was first, of course, you know,
    I couldn't well decline."

" No doubt," said I, " they settled who
    Was fittest to be sent :
Yet still to choose a brat like you,
To haunt a man of forty-two,
    Was no great compliment ! "

" I'm not so young, Sir," he replied,
    " As you might think.   The fact is,
In caverns by the water-side,
And other places that I 've tried,
    I 've had a lot of practice :

" But I have never taken yet
    A strict domestic part,
And in my flurry I forget
The Five Good Rules of Etiquette
    We have to know by heart."

"IN CAVERNS BY THE WATER-SIDE"

The Trystyng

My sympathies were warming fast
   Towards the little fellow :
He was so utterly aghast
At having found a Man at last,
   And looked so scared and yellow.

" At least," I said, " I 'm glad to find
   A Ghost is not a *dumb* thing !
But pray sit down : you 'll feel inclined
(If, like myself, you have not dined)
   To take a snack of something :

" Though, certainly, you don't appear
   A thing to offer *food* to !
And then I shall be glad to hear—
If you will say them loud and clear—
   The Rules that you allude to."

The Trystyng

" Thanks !   You shall hear them by and by.
        This *is* a piece of luck ! "
" What may I offer you ? " said I.
" Well, since you *are* so kind, I 'll try
        A little bit of duck.

" *One* slice !   And may I ask you for
        Another drop of gravy ? "
I sat and looked at him in awe,
For certainly I never saw
        A thing so white and wavy.

And still he seemed to grow more white,
        More vapoury, and wavier—
Seen in the dim and flickering light,
As he proceeded to recite
        His " Maxims of Behaviour."

Canto II

Hys Fyve Rules

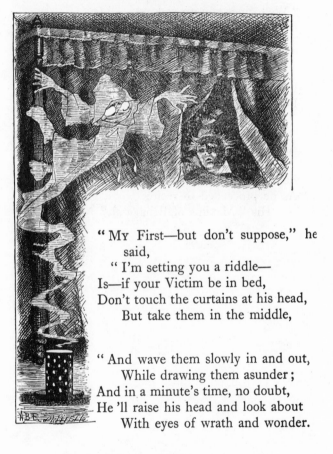

"My First—but don't suppose," he
          said,
    "I'm setting you a riddle—
Is—if your Victim be in bed,
Don't touch the curtains at his head,
    But take them in the middle,

"And wave them slowly in and out,
    While drawing them asunder;
And in a minute's time, no doubt,
He 'll raise his head and look about
    With eyes of wrath and wonder.

"And here you must on no pretence
Make the first observation.

122

Hys Fyve Rules

Wait for the Victim to commence :
No Ghost of any common sense
    Begins a conversation.

" If he should say ' *How came you here?* '
    (The way that *you* began, Sir,)
In such a case your course is clear—
' *On the bat's back, my little dear!* '
    Is the appropriate answer.

" If after this he says no more,
    You 'd best perhaps curtail your
Exertions—go and shake the door,
And then, if he begins to snore,
    You 'll know the thing 's a failure.

" By day, if he should be alone—
    At home or on a walk—
You merely give a hollow groan,
To indicate the kind of tone
    In which you mean to talk.

" But if you find him with his friends,
    The thing is rather harder.
In such a case success depends
On picking up some candle-ends,
    Or butter, in the larder.

" With this you make a kind of slide
    (It answers best with suet),
On which you must contrive to glide,

"AND SWING YOURSELF FROM SIDE TO SIDE"

Hys Fyve Rules

And swing yourself from side to side—
    One soon learns how to do it.

" The Second tells us what is right
    In ceremonious calls :—
' *First burn a blue or crimson light* '
(A thing I quite forgot to-night),
    ' *Then scratch the door or walls.*' "

I said " You 'll visit *here* no more,
    If you attempt the Guy.
I 'll have no bonfires on *my* floor—
And, as for scratching at the door,
    I 'd like to see you try ! "

" The Third was written to protect
    The interests of the Victim,
And tells us, as I recollect,
To treat him with a grave respect,
    And not to contradict him."

" That 's plain," said I, " as Tare and **Tret**,
    To any comprehension :
I only wish *some* Ghosts I 've met
Would not so *constantly* forget
    The maxim that you mention ! "

" Perhaps," he said, " *you* first transgressed
    The laws of hospitality :
All Ghosts instinctively detest
The Man that fails to treat his guest
    With proper cordiality.

" If you address a Ghost as ' Thing ! '
    Or strike him with a hatchet,
He is permitted by the King

To drop all *formal* parleying—
    And then you 're *sure* to catch it !

" The Fourth prohibits trespassing
    Where other Ghosts are quartered :
And those convicted of the thing
(Unless when pardoned by the King)
    Must instantly be slaughtered.

" That simply means ' be cut up small ' :
    Ghosts soon unite anew :
The process scarcely hurts at all—
Not more than when *you* 're what you call
    ' Cut up ' by a Review.

Hys Fyve Rules

" The Fifth is one you may prefer
    That I should quote entire :—
The King must be addressed as ' Sir.'
This, from a simple courtier,
    Is all the Laws require :

" *But, should you wish to do the thing*
    With out-and-out politeness,
Accost him as ' My Goblin King !'
And always use, in answering,
    The phrase ' Your Royal Whiteness !'

" I 'm getting rather hoarse, I fear,
    After so much reciting :
So, if you don't object, my dear,
We 'll try a glass of bitter beer—
    I think it looks inviting."

CANTO III

Scarmoges

"AND did you really walk," said I,
    " On such a wretched night ?
I always fancied Ghosts could fly—
If not exactly in the sky,
    Yet at a fairish height."

128

Scarmoges

" It 's very well," said he, " for Kings
    To soar above the earth :
But Phantoms often find that wings—
Like many other pleasant things—
    Cost more than they are worth.

" Spectres of course are rich, and so
    Can buy them from the Elves :
But *we* prefer to keep below—
They're stupid company, you know,
    For any but themselves :

" For, though they claim to be exempt
    From pride, they treat a Phantom
As something quite beneath contempt—
Just as no Turkey ever dreamt
    Of noticing a Bantam."

" They seem too proud," said I, " to go
    To houses such as mine.
Pray, how did they contrive to know
So quickly that ' the place was low,'
    And that I ' kept bad wine ' ? "

" Inspector Kobold came to you—"
    The little Ghost began.
Here I broke in—" Inspector who ?
Inspecting Ghosts is something new !
    Explain yourself, my man ! "

" His name is Kobold," said my guest :
    " One of the Spectre order :
You 'll very often see him dressed

"AND HERE HE TOOK THE FORM OF *THIRST*"

Scarmoges

In a yellow gown, a crimson vest,
  And a night-cap with a border.

" He tried the Brocken business first,
  But caught a sort of chill ;
So came to England to be nursed,
And here it took the form of *thirst*,
  Which he complains of still.

" Port-wine, he says, when rich and sound,
  Warms his old bones like nectar :
And as the inns, where it is found,
Are his especial hunting-ground,
  We call him the *Inn-Spectre*."

I bore it—bore it like a man—
  This agonizing witticism !
And nothing could be sweeter than
My temper, till the Ghost began
  Some most provoking criticism.

" Cooks need not be indulged in waste ;
  Yet still you 'd better teach them
Dishes should have *some sort* of taste.
Pray, why are all the cruets placed
  Where nobody can reach them ?

" That man of yours will never earn
  His living as a waiter !
Is that queer *thing* supposed to burn ?
(It 's far too dismal a concern
  To call a Moderator.)

" The duck was tender, but the peas
  Were very much too old :

Scarmoges

And just remember, if you please,
The *next* time you have toasted cheese,
    Don't let them send it cold.

" You 'd find the bread improved, I think,
    By getting better flour :
And have you anything to drink
That looks a *little* less like ink,
    And isn't *quite* so sour ? "

Then, peering round with curious eyes,
    He muttered " Goodness gracious ! '
And so went on to criticize—
" Your room 's an inconvenient size :
    It 's neither snug nor spacious.

" That narrow window, I expect,
    Serves but to let the dusk in—"
" But please," said I, " to recollect
'Twas fashioned by an architect
    Who pinned his faith on Ruskin ! "

" I don't care who he was, Sir, or
    On whom he pinned his faith !
Constructed by whatever law,
So poor a job I never saw,
    As I 'm a living Wraith !

" What a re-markable cigar !
    How much are they a dozen ? "
I growled " No matter what they are !
You 're getting as familiar
    As if you were my cousin !

Scarmoges

" Now that 's a thing *I will not stand,*
    And so I tell you flat."
" Aha," said he, " we 're getting grand ! "
(Taking a bottle in his hand)
    " I 'll soon arrange for *that !* "

And here he took a careful aim,
    And gaily cried " Here goes ! "
I tried to dodge it as it came,
But somehow caught it, all the same,
    Exactly on my nose.

And I remember nothing more
    That I can clearly fix,
Till I was sitting on the floor,
Repeating " Two and five are four,
    But *five and two* are six."

What really passed I never learned,
    Nor guessed : I only know
That, when at last my sense returned,
The lamp, neglected, dimly burned—
    The fire was getting low—

Through driving mists I seemed to see
    A Thing that smirked and smiled :
And found that he was giving me
A lesson in Biography,
    As if I were a child.

CANTO IV

Ibys Mouryture

"OH, when I was a little Ghost,
　　A merry time had we !
Each seated on his favourite post,
We chumped and chawed the but-
　　　tered toast
　　They gave us for our tea."

"That story is in print ! " I cried.
　　" Don't say it 's not, because
It 's known as well as Bradshaw's
　　　Guide ! "
(The Ghost uneasily replied
　　He hardly thought it was.)

"It 's not in Nursery Rhymes ?　And yet
　　I almost think it is—
' Three little Ghosteses ' were set

Hys Nouryture

'On posteses,' you know, and ate
 Their 'buttered toasteses.'

"I have the book; so if you doubt it—"
 I turned to search the shelf.
"Don't stir!" he cried. "We'll do without it:
I now remember all about it;
 I wrote the thing myself.

"It came out in a 'Monthly,' or
 At least my agent said it did:
Some literary swell, who saw
It, thought it seemed adapted for
 The Magazine he edited.

"My father was a Brownie, Sir;
 My mother was a Fairy.
The notion had occurred to her,
The children would be happier,
 If they were taught to vary.

"The notion soon became a craze;
 And, when it once began, she
Brought us all out in different ways—
One was a Pixy, two were Fays,
 Another was a Banshee;

"The Fetch and Kelpie went to school
 And gave a lot of trouble;
Next came a Poltergeist and Ghoul,
And then two Trolls (which broke the rule),
 A Goblin, and a Double—

"(If that's a snuff-box on the shelf,"
 He added with a yawn,

135

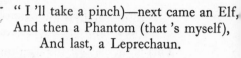

"I'll take a pinch)—next came an Elf,
    And then a Phantom (that's myself),
        And last, a Leprechaun.

"One day, some Spectres chanced to call,
    Dressed in the usual white:
I stood and watched them in the hall,
And couldn't make them out at all,
    They seemed so strange a sight.

"I wondered what on earth they were,
    That looked all head and sack;
But Mother told me not to stare,
And then she twitched me by the hair,
    And punched me in the back.

"Since then I've often wished that I
    Had been a Spectre born.
But what's the use?" (He heaved a sigh.)
"*They* are the ghost-nobility,
    And look on *us* with scorn.

"My phantom-life was soon begun:
    When I was barely six,
I went out with an older one—
And just at first I thought it fun,
    And learned a lot of tricks.

"I've haunted dungeons, castles, towers—
    Wherever I was sent:
I've often sat and howled for hours,
Drenched to the skin with driving showers,
    Upon a battlement.

Hys Nouryture

" It 's quite old-fashioned now to groan
    When you begin to speak :
This is the newest thing in tone—"
And here (it chilled me to the bone)
    He gave an *awful* squeak.

" Perhaps," he added, " to *your* ear
    That sounds an easy thing ?
Try it yourself, my little dear !
It took *me* something like a year,
    With constant practising.

" And when you 've learned to squeak, my man,
    And caught the double sob,
You 're pretty much where you began :
Just try and gibber if you can !
    That 's something *like* a job !

" *I've* tried it, and can only say
    I 'm sure you couldn't do it, e-
ven if you practised night and day,
Unless you have a turn that way,
    And natural ingenuity.

" Shakspeare I think it is who treats
    Of Ghosts, in days of old,
Who ' gibbered in the Roman streets,'
Dressed, if you recollect, in sheets—
    They must have found it cold.

" I 've often spent ten pounds on stuff,
    In dressing as a Double ;
But, though it answers as a puff,
It never has effect enough
    To make it worth the trouble.

Hys Nouryture

" Long bills soon quenched the little thirst
    I had for being funny.
The setting-up is always worst :
Such heaps of things you want at first,
    One must be made of money !

" For instance, take a Haunted Tower,
    With skull, cross-bones, and sheet ;
Blue lights to burn (say) two an hour,
Condensing lens of extra power,
    And set of chains complete :

" What with the things you have to hire—
    The fitting on the robe—
And testing all the coloured fire—
The outfit of itself would tire
    The patience of a Job !

Hys Nouryture

" And then they 're so fastidious,
 The Haunted-House Committee :
I 've often known them make a fuss
Because a Ghost was French, or Russ,
 Or even from the City !

" Some dialects are objected to—
 For one, the *Irish* brogue is :
And then, for all you have to do,
One pound a week they offer you,
 And find yourself in Bogies ! "

Canto V

Byckerment

" Don't they consult the ' Victims,' though ? "
    I said. " They should, by rights,
Give them a chance—because, you know,
The tastes of people differ so,
    Especially in Sprites."

The Phantom shook his head and smiled.
    " Consult them ? Not a bit !
'Twould be a job to drive one wild,
To satisfy one single child—
    There 'd be no end to it ! "

" Of course you can't leave *children* free,"
    Said I, " to pick and choose :
But, in the case of men like me,
I think ' Mine Host ' might fairly be
    Allowed to state his views."

He said " It really wouldn't pay—
    Folk are so full of fancies.
We visit for a single day,
And whether then we go, or stay,
    Depends on circumstances.

" And, though we don't consult ' Mine Host '
    Before the thing 's arranged,
Still, if he often quits his post,
Or is not a well-mannered Ghost,
    Then you can have him changed.

Byckerment

" But if the host 's a man like you—
    I mean a man of sense ;
And if the house is not too new—"
" Why, what has *that*," said I, " to do
    With Ghost's convenience ? "

" A new house does not suit, you know—
    It 's such a job to trim it :
But, after twenty years or so,
The wainscotings begin to go,
    So twenty is the limit."

" To trim " was not a phrase I could
    Remember having heard :
" Perhaps," I said, " you 'll be so good
As tell me what is understood
    Exactly by that word ? "

Byckerment

" It means the loosening all the doors,"
        The Ghost replied, and laughed :
" It means the drilling holes by scores
In all the skirting-boards and floors,
        To make a thorough draught.

" You 'll sometimes find that one or two
        Are all you really need
To let the wind come whistling through—
But *here* there 'll be a lot to do ! "
        I faintly gasped " Indeed !

" If I 'd been rather later, I 'll
        Be bound," I added, trying
(Most unsuccessfully) to smile,
" You 'd have been busy all this while,
        Trimming and beautifying ? "

" Why, no," said he ; " perhaps I should
        Have stayed another minute—
But still no Ghost, that 's any good,
Without an introduction would
        Have ventured to begin it.

" The proper thing, as you were late,
        Was certainly to go :
But, with the roads in such a state,
I got the Knight-Mayor's leave to wait
        For half an hour or so."

" Who 's the Knight-Mayor ? " I cried.   Instead
        Of answering my question,
" Well, if you don't know *that*," he said,
" Either you never go to bed,
        Or you 've a grand digestion !
142

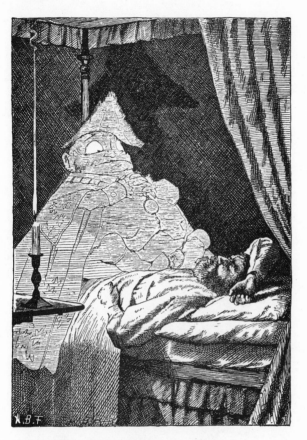

" He goes about and sits on folk
    That eat too much at night :
His duties are to pinch, and poke,
And squeeze them till they nearly choke."
    (I said " It serves them right ! ")

" And folk who sup on things like these—"
    He muttered, " eggs and bacon—
Lobster—and duck—and toasted cheese—

143

Byckerment

If they don't get an awful squeeze,
    I 'm very much mistaken !

" He is immensely fat, and so
    Well suits the occupation :
In point of fact, if you must know,
We used to call him years ago,
    The Mayor and Corporation !

" The day he was elected Mayor
    I *know* that every Sprite meant
To vote for *me*, but did not dare—
He was so frantic with despair
    And furious with excitement.

" When it was over, for a whim,
    He ran to tell the King;

Byckerment

And being the reverse of slim,
A two-mile trot was not for him
    A very easy thing.

" So, to reward him for his run
    (As it was baking hot,
And he was over twenty stone),
The King proceeded, half in fun,
    To knight him on the spot."

" 'Twas a great liberty to take ! "
    (I fired up like a rocket.)
" He did it just for punning's sake :
' The man,' says Johnson, ' that would make
    A pun, would pick a pocket ! ' "

" A man," said he, " is not a King."
    I argued for a while,
And did my best to prove the thing—
The Phantom merely listening
    With a contemptuous smile.

At last, when, breath and patience spent,
    I had recourse to smoking—
" Your *aim*," he said, " is excellent :
But—when you call it *argument*—
    Of course you 're only joking ? "

Stung by his cold and snaky eye,
    I roused myself at length
To say, " At least I do defy
The veriest sceptic to deny
    That union is strength ! "

Byckerment

" That 's true enough," said he, " yet stay—"
  I listened in all meekness—
" *Union* is strength, I 'm bound to say ;
In fact, the thing 's as clear as day ;
  But *onions* are a weakness."

CANTO VI

Dyscomfyture

As one who strives a hill to climb,
   Who never climbed before :
Who finds it, in a little time,
Grow every moment less sublime,
   And votes the thing a bore :

Yet, having once begun to try,
   Dares not desert his quest,
But, climbing, ever keeps his eye
On one small hut against the sky
   Wherein he hopes to rest :

Who climbs till nerve and force are spent,
   With many a puff and pant :
Who still, as rises the ascent,
In language grows more violent,
   Although in breath more scant :

Who, climbing, gains at length the place
   That crowns the upward track :
And, entering with unsteady pace,

Dyscomfyture

Receives a buffet in the face
  That lands him on his back :

And feels himself, like one in sleep,
  Glide swiftly down again,
A helpless weight, from steep to steep,
Till, with a headlong giddy sweep,
  He drops upon the plain—

So I, that had resolved to bring
  Conviction to a ghost,
And found it quite a different thing
From any human arguing,
  Yet dared not quit my post.

But, keeping still the end in view
  To which I hoped to come,
I strove to prove the matter true
By putting everything I knew
  Into an axiom :

Commencing every single phrase
  With " therefore " or " because,"
I blindly reeled, a hundred ways,
About the syllogistic maze,
  Unconscious where I was.

Quoth he " That 's regular clap-trap :
  Don't bluster any more.
Now *do* be cool and take a nap !
Such a ridiculous old chap
  Was never seen before !

" You 're like a man I used to meet,
  Who got one day so furious
148

In arguing, the simple heat
Scorched both his slippers off his feet!"
   I said " *That's very curious!* "

"Well, it *is* curious, I agree,
   And sounds perhaps like fibs :
But still it's true as true can be—
As sure as your name's Tibbs," said he.
   I said " My name's *not* Tibbs."

Dyscomfyture

" *Not* Tibbs ! " he cried—his tone became
        A shade or two less hearty—
" Why, no," said I.   " My proper name
Is Tibbets—"   " Tibbets ? "   " Aye, the same."
        " Why, then YOU 'RE NOT THE PARTY ! "

With that he struck the board a blow
        That shivered half the glasses.
" Why couldn't you have told me so
Three quarters of an hour ago,
        You prince of all the asses ?

" To walk four miles through mud and rain,
        To spend the night in smoking,
And then to find that it 's in vain—
And I 've to do it all again—
        It 's really *too* provoking !

" Don't talk ! " he cried, as I began
        To mutter some excuse.
" Who can have patience with a man
That 's got no more discretion than
        An idiotic goose ?

" To keep me waiting here, instead
        Of telling me at once
That this was not the house ! " he said.
" There, that 'll do—be off to bed !
        Don't gape like that, you dunce ! "

" It 's very fine to throw the blame
        On *me* in such a fashion !

Dyscomfyture

Why didn't you enquire my name
The very minute that you came ? "
    I answered in a passion.

  " Of course it worries you a bit
      To come so far on foot—
But how was *I* to blame for it ? "
" Well, well ! " said he. " I must admit
      That isn't badly put.

Dyscomfyture

" And certainly you 've given me
    The best of wine and victual—
Excuse my violence," said he,
" But accidents like this, you see,
    They put one out a little.

" 'Twas *my* fault after all, I find—
    Shake hands, old Turnip-top ! "
The name was hardly to my mind,
But, as no doubt he meant it kind,
    I let the matter drop.

" Good-night, old Turnip-top, good-night !
    When I am gone, perhaps
They 'll send you some inferior Sprite,
Who 'll keep you in a constant fright
    And spoil your soundest naps.

" Tell him you 'll stand no sort of trick ;
    Then, if he leers and chuckles,
You just be handy with a stick
(Mind that it 's pretty hard and thick)
    And rap him on the knuckles !

" Then carelessly remark ' Old coon !
    Perhaps you're not aware
That, if you don't behave, you'll soon
Be chuckling to another tune—
    And so you 'd best take care ! '

Dyscomfyture

"That's the right way to cure a Sprite
    Of such-like goings-on—
But gracious me! It's getting light!
Good-night, old Turnip-top, good-night!"
    A nod, and he was gone.

Sad Souvenaunce

"What's this?" I pondered. "Have I slept?
    Or can I have been drinking?"
But soon a gentler feeling crept
Upon me, and I sat and wept
    An hour or so, like winking.

"No need for Bones to hurry so!"
    I sobbed. "In fact, I doubt
If it was worth his while to go—
And who is Tibbs, I'd like to know,
    To make such work about?

154

"If Tibbs is anything like me,
    It 's *possible*," I said,
"He won't be over-pleased to be
Dropped in upon at half-past three,
    After he 's snug in bed.

"And if Bones plagues him anyhow—
    Squeaking and all the rest of it,
As he was doing here just now—

Sad Souvenaunce

I prophesy there 'll be a row,
  And Tibbs will have the best of it ! "

Then, as my tears could never bring
  The friendly Phantom back,
It seemed to me the proper thing
To mix another glass, and sing
  The following Coronach.

And art thou gone, beloved Ghost ?
  Best of Familiars !
Nay then, farewell, my duckling roast,
Farewell, farewell, my tea and toast,
  My meerschaum and cigars !

The hues of life are dull and gray,
  The sweets of life insipid,
When thou, *my charmer, art away—*
Old Brick, or rather, let me say,
  Old Parallelepiped ! "

Instead of singing Verse the Third,
  I ceased—abruptly, rather :
But, after such a splendid word
I felt that it would be absurd
  To try it any farther.

So with a yawn I went my way
  To seek the welcome downy,
And slept, and dreamed till break of day
Of Poltergeist and Fetch and Fay
  And Leprechaun and Brownie !

Sad Souvenaunce

For years I've not been visited
  By any kind of Sprite;
Yet still they echo in my head,
Those parting words, so kindly said,
  " Old Turnip-top, good-night ! "

ECHOES

LADY Clara Vere de Vere
Was eight years old, she said :
Every ringlet, lightly shaken, ran itself in golden
thread.

She took her little porringer :
Of me she shall not win renown :
For the baseness of its nature shall have strength to
drag her down.

" Sisters and brothers, little Maid ?
There stands the Inspector at thy door :
Like a dog, he hunts for boys who know not two and
two are four."

" Kind hearts are more than coronets,"
She said, and wondering looked at me :
" It is the dead unhappy night, and I must hurry
home to tea."

A SEA DIRGE

THERE are certain things—as, a spider, a ghost,
  The income-tax, gout, an umbrella for three—
That I hate, but the thing that I hate the most
    Is a thing they call the Sea.

Pour some salt water over the floor—
  Ugly I'm sure you'll allow it to be :
Suppose it extended a mile or more,
    That's very like the Sea.

Beat a dog till it howls outright—
  Cruel, but all very well for a spree :
Suppose that he did so day and night,
    That would be like the Sea.

I had a vision of nursery-maids ;
  Tens of thousands passed by me—

A Sea Dirge

All leading children with wooden spades,
    And this was by the Sea.

Who invented those spades of wood?
  Who was it cut them out of the tree?
None, I think, but an idiot could—
    Or one that loved the Sea.

It is pleasant and dreamy, no doubt, to float
  With "thoughts as boundless, and souls as free":
But, suppose you are very unwell in the boat,
    How do you like the Sea?

There is an insect that people avoid
  (Whence is derived the verb "to flee").
Where have you been by it most annoyed?
    In lodgings by the Sea.

If you like your coffee with sand for dregs,
  A decided hint of salt in your tea,
And a fishy taste in the very eggs—
    By all means choose the Sea.

And if, with these dainties to drink and eat,
  You prefer not a vestige of grass or tree,
And a chronic state of wet in your feet,
    Then—I recommend the Sea.

For *I* have friends who dwell by the coast—
  Pleasant friends they are to me!
It is when I am with them I wonder most
    That anyone likes the Sea.

They take me a walk: though tired and stiff,
  To climb the heights I madly agree;

A Sea Dirge

And, after a tumble or so from the cliff,
   They kindly suggest the Sea.

I try the rocks, and I think it cool
   That they laugh with such an excess of glee,
As I heavily slip into every pool
   That skirts the cold cold Sea.

Ye Carpette Knyghte

I habe a horse—a ryghte goode horse—
Ne doe I enbye those
Who scoure ye playne yn headye course
Tyll soddayne on theyre nose
They lyghte wyth unexpected force—
Yt ys—a horse of clothes.

Ye Carpette Knyghte

I habe a saddel—"Say'st thou soe?
　　Wyth styrruppes, Knyghte, to boote?"
I sayde not that—I answere "Noe"—
　　Yt lacketh such, I woote:
Yt ys a mutton-saddel, loe!
　　Parte of ye fleecye brute.

I habe a bytte—a ryghte good bytte—
　　As shall bee seene yn tyme.
Y^e jawe of horse yt wyll not fytte;
　　Yts use ys more sublyme.
Fayre Syr, how deemest thou of yt?
　　Yt ys—thys bytte of rhyme.

HIAWATHA'S PHOTOGRAPHING

[In an age of imitation, I can claim no special merit
for this slight attempt at doing what is known to be
so easy.   Any fairly practised writer, with the slightest
ear for rhythm, could compose, for hours together, in
the easy running metre of " The Song of Hiawatha."
Having, then, distinctly stated that I challenge no
attention in the following little poem to its merely
verbal jingle, I must beg the candid reader to confine
his criticism to its treatment of the subject.[1]]

FROM his shoulder Hiawatha
Took the camera of rosewood,
Made of sliding, folding rosewood ;
Neatly put it all together.
In its case it lay compactly,
Folded into nearly nothing ;
But he opened out the hinges,
Pushed and pulled the joints and hinges,
Till it looked all squares and oblongs,
Like a complicated figure
In the Second Book of Euclid.

[1] It may be noted that this "prose" introduction is also in the
Hiawatha metre.

Hiawatha's Photographing

This he perched upon a tripod—
Crouched beneath its dusky cover—
Stretched his hand, enforcing silence—
Said, " Be motionless, I beg you ! "
Mystic, awful was the process.

All the family in order
Sat before him for their pictures :
Each in turn, as he was taken,
Volunteered his own suggestions,
His ingenious suggestions.
First the Governor, the Father :
He suggested velvet curtains
Looped about a massy pillar ;
And the corner of a table,
Of a rosewood dining-table.
He would hold a scroll of something,

Hiawatha's Photographing

Hold it firmly in his left-hand ;
He would keep his right-hand buried

(Like Napoleon) in his waistcoat ;
He would contemplate the distance

Hiawatha's Photographing

With a look of pensive meaning,
As of ducks that die in tempests.
    Grand, heroic was the notion :
Yet the picture failed entirely :
Failed, because he moved a little,
Moved, because he couldn't help it.
    Next, his better half took courage ;
She would have her picture taken.
She came dressed beyond description,
Dressed in jewels and in satin
Far too gorgeous for an empress.
Gracefully she sat down sideways,
With a simper scarcely human,
Holding in her hand a bouquet
Rather larger than a cabbage.
All the while that she was sitting,
Still the lady chattered, chattered,
Like a monkey in the forest.
" Am I sitting still ? " she asked him.
" Is my face enough in profile ?
Shall I hold the bouquet higher ?
Will it come into the picture ? "
And the picture failed completely.
    Next the Son, the Stunning-Cantab :
He suggested curves of beauty,
Curves pervading all his figure,
Which the eye might follow onward,
Till they centered in the breast-pin,
Centered in the golden breast-pin.
He had learnt it all from Ruskin
(Author of " The Stones of Venice,"
" Seven Lamps of Architecture,"

Hiawatha's Photographing

"Modern Painters," and some others);
And perhaps he had not fully

Understood his author's meaning;
But, whatever was the reason,

Hiawatha's Photographing

All was fruitless, as the picture
Ended in an utter failure.

Next to him the eldest daughter :
She suggested very little,

Hiawatha's Photographing

Only asked if he would take her
With her look of " passive beauty."
   Her idea of passive beauty
Was a squinting of the left-eye,
Was a drooping of the right-eye,
Was a smile that went up sideways
To the corner of the nostrils.
   Hiawatha, when she asked him,
Took no notice of the question,
Looked as if he hadn't heard it ;
But, when pointedly appealed to,
Smiled in his peculiar manner,
Coughed and said it " didn't matter,"
Bit his lip and changed the subject.
   Nor in this was he mistaken,
As the picture failed completely.
   So in turn the other sisters.
   Last, the youngest son was taken :
Very rough and thick his hair was,
Very round and red his face was,
Very dusty was his jacket,
Very fidgety his manner.
And his overbearing sisters
Called him names he disapproved of :
Called him Johnny, " Daddy's Darling,"
Called him Jacky, " Scrubby School-boy."
And, so awful was the picture,
In comparison the others
Seemed, to one's bewildered fancy,
To have partially succeeded.
   Finally my Hiawatha
Tumbled all the tribe together,

("Grouped" is not the right expression),
And, as happy chance would have it

Did at last obtain a picture
Where the faces all succeeded:

Hiawatha's Photographing

Each came out a perfect likeness.
  Then they joined and all abused it,
Unrestrainedly abused it,
As the worst and ugliest picture
They could possibly have dreamed of.
" Giving one such strange expressions—
Sullen, stupid, pert expressions.
Really any one would take us
(Any one that did not know us)
For the most unpleasant people ! "
(Hiawatha seemed to think so,
Seemed to think it not unlikely).
All together rang their voices,
Angry, loud, discordant voices,
As of dogs that howl in concert,
As of cats that wail in chorus.
  But my Hiawatha's patience,
His politeness and his patience,
Unaccountably had vanished,
And he left that happy party.
Neither did he leave them slowly,
With the calm deliberation,
The intense deliberation
Of a photographic artist :
But he left them in a hurry,
Left them in a mighty hurry,
Stating that he would not stand it,
Stating in emphatic language
What he'd be before he'd stand it.
Hurriedly he packed his boxes :
Hurriedly the porter trundled
On a barrow all his boxes :

Hiawatha's Photographing

Hurriedly he took his ticket :
Hurriedly the train received him :
Thus departed Hiawatha.

MELANCHOLETTA

WITH saddest music all day long
   She soothed her secret sorrow :
At night she sighed " I fear 'twas wrong
   Such cheerful words to borrow.
Dearest, a sweeter, sadder song
   I'll sing to thee to-morrow."

I thanked her, but I could not say
   That I was glad to hear it :
I left the house at break of day,
   And did not venture near it
Till time, I hoped, had worn away
   Her grief, for nought could cheer it !

Melancholetta

My dismal sister ! Couldst thou know
  The wretched home thou keepest !
Thy brother, drowned in daily woe,

  Is thankful when thou sleepest ;
For if I laugh, however low,
  When thou'rt awake, thou weepest !

175

Melancholetta

I took my sister t'other day
  (Excuse the slang expression)
To Sadler's Wells to see the play
  In hopes the new impression
Might in her thoughts, from grave to gay
  Effect some slight digression.

I asked three gay young dogs from town
  To join us in our folly,
Whose mirth, I thought, might serve to drown
  My sister's melancholy :
The lively Jones, the sportive Brown,
  And Robinson the jolly.

The maid announced the meal in tones
  That I myself had taught her,
Meant to allay my sister's moans
  Like oil on troubled water :
I rushed to Jones, the lively Jones,
  And begged him to escort her.

Vainly he strove, with ready wit,
  To joke about the weather—
To ventilate the last " *on dit* "—
  To quote the price of leather—
She groaned " Here I and Sorrow sit :
  Let us lament together ! "

I urged " You're wasting time, you know :
  Delay will spoil the venison."
" My heart is wasted with my woe !
  There is no rest—in Venice, on
The Bridge of Sighs ! " she quoted low
  From Byron and from Tennyson.

176

Melancholetta

I need not tell of soup and fish
   In solemn silence swallowed,
The sobs that ushered in each dish,
   And its departure followed,
Nor yet my suicidal wish
   To *be* the cheese I hollowed.

Some desperate attempts were made
   To start a conversation ;
" Madam," the sportive Brown essayed,
   " Which kind of recreation,
Hunting or fishing, have you made
   Your special occupation ? "

Her lips curved downwards instantly,
   As if of india-rubber.
" Hounds *in full cry* I like," said she :
   (Oh, how I longed to snub her !)
" Of fish, a whale's the one for me,
   It is so full of blubber ! "

The night's performance was " King John."
   " It's dull," she wept, " and so-so ! "
Awhile I let her tears flow on,
   She said they soothed her woe so !
At length the curtain rose upon
   " Bombastes Furioso."

In vain we roared ; in vain we tried
   To rouse her into laughter :
Her pensive glances wandered wide
   From orchestra to rafter—
" *Tier upon tier !* " she said, and sighed ;
   And silence followed after.

177

A VALENTINE

[Sent to a friend who had complained that I was glad enough to see him when he came, but didn't seem to miss him if he stayed away.]

AND cannot pleasures, while they last,
Be actual unless, when past,
They leave us shuddering and aghast,
    With anguish smarting?
And cannot friends be firm and fast,
    And yet bear parting?

And must I then, at Friendship's call,
Calmly resign the little all
(Trifling, I grant, it is and small)
    I have of gladness,
And lend my being to the thrall
    Of gloom and sadness?

And think you that I should be dumb,
And full *dolorum omnium,*
Excepting when *you* choose to come
    And share my dinner?
At other times be sour and glum
    And daily thinner?

A Valentine

Must he then only live to weep,
Who'd prove his friendship true and deep,
By day a lonely shadow creep,
    At night-time languish,
Oft raising in his broken sleep
    The moan of anguish?

The lover, if for certain days
His fair one be denied his gaze,
Sinks not in grief and wild amaze,
    But, wiser wooer,
He spends the time in writing lays,
    And posts them to her.

And if the verse flow free and fast,
Till even the poet is aghast,
A touching Valentine at last
    The post shall carry,
When thirteen days are gone and past
    Of February.

Farewell, dear friend, and when we meet,
In desert waste or crowded street,
Perhaps before this week shall fleet,
    Perhaps to-morrow,
I trust to find *your* heart the seat
    Of wasting sorrow.

THE THREE VOICES

Ţhe First Voice

HE trilled a carol fresh and free,
He laughed aloud for very glee :
There came a breeze from off the sea :

It passed athwart the glooming flat—
It fanned his forehead as he sat—
It lightly bore away his hat,

All to the feet of one who stood
Like maid enchanted in a wood,
Frowning as darkly as she could.

With huge umbrella, lank and brown,
Unerringly she pinned it down,
Right through the centre of the crown.

180

The Three Voices

Then, with an aspect cold and grim,
Regardless of its battered rim,
She took it up and gave it him.

A while like one in dreams he stood,
Then faltered forth his gratitude
In words just short of being rude :

For it had lost its shape and shine,
And it had cost him four-and-nine,
And he was going out to dine.

" To dine ! " she sneered in acid tone,
" To bend thy being to a bone
Clothed in a radiance not its own ! "

The tear-drop trickled to his chin :
There was a meaning in her grin
That made him feel on fire within.

" Term it not ' radiance,' " said he :
" 'Tis solid nutriment to me.
Dinner is Dinner : Tea is Tea."

And she, " Yea so ?   Yet wherefore cease ?
Let thy scant knowledge find increase.
Say ' Men are Men, and Geese are Geese.' "

He moaned : he knew not what to say.
The thought " That I could get away ! "
Strove with the thought " But I must stay."

The Three Voices

" To dine ! " she shrieked in dragon-wrath.
" To swallow wines all foam and froth !
To simper at a table-cloth !

" Say, can thy noble spirit stoop
To join the gormandising troop
Who find a solace in the soup ?

" Canst thou desire or pie or puff ?
Thy well-bred manners were enough,
Without such gross material stuff."

" Yet well-bred men," he faintly said,
" Are not unwilling to be fed :
Nor are they well without the bread."

Her visage scorched him ere she spoke :
" There are," she said, " a kind of folk
Who have no horror of a joke.

" Such wretches live : they take their share
Of common earth and common air :
We come across them here and there :

" We grant them—there is no escape—
A sort of semi-human shape
Suggestive of the man-like Ape."

" In all such theories," said he,
" One fixed exception there must be.
That is, the Present Company."

The Three Voices

Baffled, she gave a wolfish bark :
He, aiming blindly in the dark,
With random shaft had pierced the mark.

She felt that her defeat was plain,
Yet madly strove with might and main
To get the upper hand again.

Fixing her eyes upon the beach,
As though unconscious of his speech,
She said " Each gives to more than each."

He could not answer yea or nay :
He faltered " Gifts may pass away."
Yet knew not what he meant to say.

" If that be so," she straight replied,
" Each heart with each doth coincide.
What boots it ?   For the world is wide."

" The world is but a Thought," said he :
" The vast unfathomable sea
Is but a Notion—unto me."

And darkly fell her answer dread
Upon his unresisting head,
Like half a hundredweight of lead.

" The Good and Great must ever shun
That reckless and abandoned one
Who stoops to perpetrate a pun.

" The man that smokes—that reads *The Times*—
That goes to Christmas Pantomimes—
Is capable of *any* crimes ! "

183

"THIS IS HARDER THAN BEZIQUE!"

The Three Voices

He felt it was his turn to speak,
And, with a shamed and crimson cheek,
Moaned " This is harder than Bezique ! "

But when she asked him " Wherefore so ? "
He felt his very whiskers glow,
And frankly owned " I do not know."

While, like broad waves of golden grain,
Or sunlit hues on cloistered pane,
His colour came and went again.

Pitying his obvious distress,
Yet with a tinge of bitterness,
She said " The More exceeds the Less."

" A truth of such undoubted weight,"
He urged, " and so extreme in date,
It were superfluous to state."

Roused into sudden passion, she
In tone of cold malignity :
" To others, yea : but not to thee."

But when she saw him quail and quake,
And when he urged " For pity's sake ! "
Once more in gentle tones she spake.

" Thought in the mind doth still abide
That is by Intellect supplied,
And within that Idea doth hide :

" And he, that yearns the truth to know
Still further inwardly may go,
And find Idea from Notion flow :

The Three Voices

" And thus the chain, that sages sought,
Is to a glorious circle wrought,
For Notion hath its source in Thought."

So passed they on with even pace :
Yet gradually one might trace
A shadow growing on his face.

The Second Voice

THEY walked beside the wave-worn beach;
Her tongue was very apt to teach,
And now and then he did beseech

She would abate her dulcet tone,
Because the talk was all her own,
And he was dull as any drone.

She urged " No cheese is made of chalk ":
And ceaseless flowed her dreary talk,
Tuned to the footfall of a walk.

Her voice was very full and rich,
And, when at length she asked him " Which ? "
It mounted to its highest pitch.

He a bewildered answer gave,
Drowned in the sullen moaning wave,
Lost in the echoes of the cave.

He answered her he knew not what :
Like shaft from bow at random shot,
He spoke, but she regarded not.

187

The Second Voice

She waited not for his reply,
But with a downward leaden eye
Went on as if he were not by—

Sound argument and grave defence,
Strange questions raised on " Why ? " and
 " Whence ? "
And wildly tangled evidence.

When he, with racked and whirling brain,
Feebly implored her to explain,
She simply said it all again.

Wrenched with an agony intense,
He spake, neglecting Sound and Sense,
And careless of all consequence :

" Mind—I believe—is Essence—Ent—
Abstract—that is—an Accident—
Which we—that is to say—I meant——"

When, with quick breath and cheeks all flushed,
At length his speech was somewhat hushed,
She looked at him, and he was crushed.

It needed not her calm reply :
She fixed him with a stony eye,
And he could neither fight nor fly.

While she dissected, word by word,
His speech, half guessed at and half heard,
As might a cat a little bird.

Then, having wholly overthrown
His views, and stripped them to the bone,
Proceeded to unfold her own.

" Shall Man be Man ? And shall he miss
Of other thoughts no thought but this,
Harmonious dews of sober bliss ?

"SHALL MAN BE MAN?"

The Second Voice

" What boots it ?   Shall his fevered eye
Through towering nothingness descry
The grisly phantom hurry by ?

" And hear dumb shrieks that fill the air ;
See mouths that gape, and eyes that stare
And redden in the dusky glare ?

" The meadows breathing amber light,
The darkness toppling from the height,
The feathery train of granite Night ?

" Shall he, grown gray among his peers,
Through the thick curtain of his tears
Catch glimpses of his earlier years,

" And hear the sounds he knew of yore,
Old shufflings on the sanded floor,
Old knuckles tapping at the door ?

" Yet still before him as he flies
One pallid form shall ever rise,
And, bodying forth in glassy eyes

" The vision of a vanished good,
Low peering through the tangled wood,
Shall freeze the current of his blood."

Still from each fact, with skill uncouth
And savage rapture, like a tooth
She wrenched some slow reluctant truth.

Till, like a silent water-mill,
When summer suns have dried the rill,
She reached a full stop, and was still.

The Second Voice

Dead calm succeeded to the fuss,
As when the loaded omnibus
Has reached the railway terminus :

When, for the tumult of the street,
Is heard the engine's stifled beat,
The velvet tread of porters' feet.

With glance that ever sought the ground,
She moved her lips without a sound,
And every now and then she frowned.

He gazed upon the sleeping sea,
And joyed in its tranquillity,
And in that silence dead, but she

To muse a little space did seem,
Then, like the echo of a dream,
Harked back upon her threadbare theme.

Still an attentive ear he lent
But could not fathom what she meant :
She was not deep, nor eloquent.

He marked the ripple on the sand :
The even swaying of her hand
Was all that he could understand.

He saw in dreams a drawing-room,
Where thirteen wretches sat in gloom,
Waiting—he thought he knew for whom :

He saw them drooping here and there,
Each feebly huddled on a chair,
In attitudes of blank despair :

191

The Second Voice

Oysters were not more mute than they,
For all their brains were pumped away,
And they had nothing more to say—

Save one, who groaned " Three hours are gone ! "
Who shrieked " We'll wait no longer, John !
Tell them to set the dinner on ! "

The vision passed : the ghosts were fled :
He saw once more that woman dread :
He heard once more the words she said.

He left her, and he turned aside :
He sat and watched the coming tide
Across the shores so newly dried.

He wondered at the waters clear,
The breeze that whispered in his ear,
The billows heaving far and near,

And why he had so long preferred
To hang upon her every word :
" In truth," he said, " it was absurd."

The Third Voice

NOT long this transport held its place :
Within a little moment's space
Quick tears were raining down his face.

His heart stood still, aghast with fear ;
A wordless voice, nor far nor near,
He seemed to hear and not to hear.

" Tears kindle not the doubtful spark.
If so, why not ?   Of this remark
The bearings are profoundly dark."

" Her speech," he said, " hath caused this pain.
Easier I count it to explain
The jargon of the howling main,

The Third Voice

" Or, stretched beside some babbling brook,
To con, with inexpressive look,
An unintelligible book."

Low spake the voice within his head,
In words imagined more than said,
Soundless as ghost's intended tread :

" If thou art duller than before,
Why quittedst thou the voice of lore ?
Why not endure, expecting more ? "

" Rather than that," he groaned aghast,
" I'd writhe in depths of cavern vast,
Some loathly vampire's rich repast."

" 'Twere hard," it answered, " themes immense
To coop within the narrow fence
That rings *thy* scant intelligence."

" Not so," he urged, " nor once alone :
But there was something in her tone
That chilled me to the very bone.

" Her style was anything but clear,
And most unpleasantly severe ;
Her epithets were very queer.

" And yet, so grand were her replies,
I could not choose but deem her wise ;
I did not dare to criticise ;

" Nor did I leave her, till she went
So deep in tangled argument
That all my powers of thought were spent."

The Third Voice

A little whisper inly slid,
" Yet truth is truth : you know you did."
A little wink beneath the lid.

And, sickened with excess of dread,
Prone to the dust he bent his head,
And lay like one three-quarters dead.

The whisper left him—like a breeze
Lost in the depths of leafy trees—
Left him by no means at his ease.

Once more he weltered in despair,
With hands, through denser-matted hair,
More tightly clenched than then they were.

When, bathed in Dawn of living red,
Majestic frowned the mountain head,
" Tell me my fault," was all he said.

When, at high Noon, the blazing sky
Scorched in his head each haggard eye,
Then keenest rose his weary cry.

And when at Eve the unpitying sun
Smiled grimly on the solemn fun,
" Alack," he sighed, " what *have* I done ? "

But saddest, darkest was the sight,
When the cold grasp of leaden Night
Dashed him to earth, and held him tight.

Tortured, unaided, and alone,
Thunders were silence to his groan,
Bagpipes sweet music to its tone :

"A SCARED DULLARD, GIBBERING LOW"

The Third Voice

" What ?   Ever thus, in dismal round,
Shall Pain and Mystery profound
Pursue me like a sleepless hound,

" With crimson-dashed and eager jaws,
Me, still in ignorance of the cause,
Unknowing what I broke of laws ? "

The whisper to his ear did seem
Like echoed flow of silent stream,
Or shadow of forgotten dream,

The whisper trembling in the wind :
" Her fate with thine was intertwined,"
So spake it in his inner mind :

" Each orbed on each a baleful star :
Each proved the other's blight and bar :
Each unto each were best, most far :

" Yea, each to each was worse than foe :
Thou, a scared dullard, gibbering low,
AND SHE, AN AVALANCHE OF WOE ! "

TÈMA CON VARIAZIONI

[WHY is it that Poetry has never yet been subjected
to that process of Dilution which has proved so ad-
vantageous to her sister-art Music? The Diluter
gives us first a few notes of some well-known Air,
then a dozen bars of his own, then a few more notes
of the Air, and so on alternately : thus saving the
listener, if not from all risk of recognising the melody
at all, at least from the too-exciting transports which
it might produce in a more concentrated form. The
process is termed " setting " by Composers, and any
one, that has ever experienced the emotion of being
unexpectedly set down in a heap of mortar, will recognise the truthfulness of this happy phrase.

For truly, just as the genuine Epicure lingers
lovingly over a morsel of supreme Venison—whose
every fibre seems to murmur " Excelsior ! "—yet
swallows, ere returning to the toothsome dainty, great
mouthfuls of oatmeal-porridge and winkles : and just
as the perfect Connoisseur in Claret permits himself
but one delicate sip, and then tosses off a pint or
more of boarding-school beer : so also——]

I NEVER loved a dear Gazelle—
    Nor anything that cost me much :
    High prices profit those who sell,
        But why should I be fond of such ?

198

Tèma Con Variaziòni

To glad me with his soft black eye
    My son comes trotting home from school ;
He's had a fight but can't tell why—
    He always was a little fool !

But, when he came to know me well,
    He kicked me out, her testy Sire :
And when I stained my hair, that Belle
    Might note the change, and thus admire

And love me, it was sure to dye
    A muddy green, or staring blue :
Whilst one might trace, with half an eye,
    The still triumphant carrot through.

A GAME OF FIVES

FIVE little girls, of Five, Four, Three, Two, One :
Rolling on the hearthrug, full of tricks and fun.

Five rosy girls, in years from Ten to Six :
Sitting down to lessons—no more time for tricks.

Five growing girls, from Fifteen to Eleven :
Music, Drawing, Languages, and food enough for
    seven !

Five winsome girls, from Twenty to Sixteen :
Each young man that calls, I say " Now tell me which
    you *mean !* "

Five dashing girls, the youngest Twenty-one :
But, if nobody proposes, what is there to be done ?

Five showy girls—but Thirty is an age
When girls may be *engaging*, but they somehow don't
    engage.

Five dressy girls, of Thirty-one or more ;

So gracious to the shy young men they snubbed so
    much before !

   *   *   *   *   *   *

Five *passé* girls—Their age ?   Well, never mind !
We jog along together, like the rest of human kind :
But the quondam " careless bachelor " begins to
    think he knows
The answer to that ancient problem " how the money
    goes " !

POETA FIT, NON NASCITUR

" How shall I be a poet ?
  How shall I write in rhyme :
You told me once ' the very wish
  Partook of the sublime.'
Then tell me how !   Don't put me off
  With your ' another time ' ! "

The old man smiled to see him,
  To hear his sudden sally ;
He liked the lad to speak his mind
  Enthusiastically ;

Poeta Fit, Non Nascitur

And thought " There's no hum-drum in him,
 Nor any shilly-shally."

" And would you be a poet
 Before you've been to school ?
Ah, well ! I hardly thought you
 So absolute a fool.
First learn to be spasmodic—
 A very simple rule.

" For first you write a sentence,
 And then you chop it small ;
Then mix the bits, and sort them out
 Just as they chance to fall :
The order of the phrases makes
 No difference at all.

" Then, if you'd be impressive,
 Remember what I say,
That abstract qualities begin
 With capitals alway :
The True, the Good, the Beautiful—
 Those are the things that pay !

" Next, when you are describing
 A shape, or sound, or tint ;
Don't state the matter plainly,
 But put it in a hint ;
And learn to look at all things
 With a sort of mental squint."

" For instance, if I wished, Sir,
 Of mutton-pies to tell,
Should I say ' dreams of fleecy flocks

Pent in a wheaten cell ' ? "
" Why, yes," the old man said : " that phrase
Would answer very well.

" Then fourthly, there are epithets
    That suit with any word—
As well as Harvey's Reading Sauce
    With fish, or flesh, or bird—
Of these, ' wild,' ' lonely,' ' weary,' ' strange,'
    Are much to be preferred."

" And will it do, O will it do
    To take them in a lump—
As ' the wild man went his weary way
    To a strange and lonely pump ' ? "
  " Nay, nay !   You must not hastily
    To such conclusions jump.

" Such epithets, like pepper,
    Give zest to what you write ;
And, if you strew them sparely,
    They whet the appetite :
But if you lay them on too thick,
    You spoil the matter quite !

" Last, as to the arrangement :
    Your reader, you should show him,
Must take what information he
    Can get, and look for no im-
mature disclosure of the drift
    And purpose of your poem.

" Therefore, to test his patience—
    How much he can endure—

Poeta Fit, Non Nascitur

Mention no places, names, or dates,
    And evermore be sure
Throughout the poem to be found
    Consistently obscure.

" First fix upon the limit
    To which it shall extend :
Then fill it up with ' Padding '
    (Beg some of any friend) :
Your great SENSATION-STANZA
    You place towards the end."

" And what is a Sensation,
    Grandfather, tell me, pray ?
I think I never heard the word
    So used before to-day :
Be kind enough to mention one
    ' *Exempli gratiâ.*' "

And the old man, looking sadly
    Across the garden-lawn,
Where here and there a dew-drop
    Yet glittered in the dawn,
Said " Go to the Adelphi,
    And see the ' Colleen Bawn.'

" The word is due to Boucicault—
    The theory is his,
Where Life becomes a Spasm,
    And History a Whiz :
If that is not Sensation,
    I don't know what it is.

" Now try your hand, ere Fancy
    Have lost its present glow——"

Poeta Fit, Non Nascitur

" And then," his grandson added,
   " We'll publish it, you know :
Green cloth—gold-lettered at the back—
   In duodecimo ! "

Then proudly smiled that old man
   To see the eager lad
Rush madly for his pen and ink
   And for his blotting-pad—
But, when he thought of *publishing*,
   His face grew stern and sad.

SIZE AND TEARS

WHEN on the sandy shore I sit,
   Beside the salt sea-wave,
And fall into a weeping fit
   Because I dare not shave—
A little whisper at my ear
Enquires the reason of my fear.

I answer " If that ruffian Jones
   Should recognise me here,
He'd bellow out my name in tones
   Offensive to the ear :
He chaffs me so on being stout
(A thing that always puts me out)."

Size and Tears

Ah me! I see him on the cliff!
   Farewell, farewell to hope,
If he should look this way, and if
   He's got his telescope!
To whatsoever place I flee,
My odious rival follows me!

For every night, and everywhere,
   I meet him out at dinner;
And when I've found some charming fair,
   And vowed to die or win her,
The wretch (he's thin and I am stout)
Is sure to come and cut me out!

The girls (just like them!) all agree
   To praise J. Jones, Esquire:
I ask them what on earth they see
   About him to admire?
They cry " He is so sleek and slim,
It's quite a treat to look at him! "

They vanish in tobacco smoke,
   Those visionary maids—
I feel a sharp and sudden poke
   Between the shoulder-blades—
" Why, Brown, my boy! You're growing stout! "
(I told you he would find me out!)

" My growth is not *your* business, Sir! "
   " No more it is, my boy!
But if it's *yours*, as I infer,
   Why, Brown, I give you joy! "

Size and Tears

A man, whose business prospers so,
Is just the sort of man to know !

" It's hardly safe, though, talking here—
  I'd best get out of reach :
For such a weight as yours, I fear,
  Must shortly sink the beach ! "—
Insult me thus because I'm stout !
I vow I'll go and call him out !

ATALANTA IN CAMDEN-TOWN

Ay, 'twas here, on this spot,
   In that summer of yore,
Atalanta did not
   Vote my presence a bore,
Nor reply to my tenderest talk " She had
  heard all that nonsense before."

She'd the brooch I had bought
   And the necklace and sash on,
And her heart, as I thought,
   Was alive to my passion ;
And she'd done up her hair in the style that
  the Empress had brought into fashion.

I had been to the play
   With my pearl of a Peri—
But, for all I could say,

Atalanta in Camden-Town

She declared she was weary,
That " the place was so crowded and hot, and
she couldn't abide that Dundreary."

Then I thought " Lucky boy !
'Tis for *you* that she whimpers ! "
And I noted with joy
Those sensational simpers :
And I said " This is scrumptious ! "—a phrase I had
learned from the Devonshire shrimpers.

And I vowed " 'Twill be said
I'm a fortunate fellow,
When the breakfast is spread,
When the topers are mellow,
When the foam of the bride-cake is white, and the
fierce orange-blossoms are yellow ! "

O that languishing yawn !
O those eloquent eyes !
I was drunk with the dawn
Of a splendid surmise—
I was stung by a look, I was slain by a tear, by a
tempest of sighs.

Then I whispered " I see
The sweet secret thou keepest.
And the yearning for *ME*
That thou wistfully weepest !
And the question is ' License or Banns ? ' though
undoubtedly Banns are the cheapest."

" Be my Hero," said I,
" And let *me* be Leander ! "

Atalanta in Camden-Town

But I lost her reply—
Something ending with "gander"—
For the omnibus rattled so loud that no mortal could quite understand her.

THE LANG COORTIN'

THE ladye she stood at her lattice high,
　Wi' her doggie at her feet ;
Thorough the lattice she can spy
　The passers in the street,

" There's one that standeth at the door,
　And tirleth at the pin :
Now speak and say, my popinjay,
　If I sall let him in."

Then up and spake the popinjay
　That flew abune her head :
" Gae let him in that tirls the pin :
　He cometh thee to wed."

O when he cam' the parlour in,
　A woeful man was he !

The Lang Coortin'

" And dinna ye ken your lover agen,
   Sae well that loveth thee ? "

" And how wad I ken ye loved me, Sir,
   That have been sae lang away ?
And how wad I ken ye loved me, Sir ?
   Ye never telled me sae."

Said—" Ladye dear," and the salt, salt tear
   Cam' rinnin' doon his cheek,
" I have sent the tokens of my love
   This many and many a week.

" O didna ye get the rings, Ladye,
   The rings o' the gowd sae fine ?
I wot that I have sent to thee
   Four score, four score and nine."

" They cam' to me," said that fair ladye.
   " Wow, they were flimsie things ! "
Said—" that chain o' gowd, my doggie to howd,
   It is made o' thae self-same rings."

" And didna ye get the locks, the locks,
   The locks o' my ain black hair,
Whilk I sent by post, whilk I sent by box,
   Whilk I sent by the carrier ? "

" They cam' to me," said that fair ladye ;
   " And I prithee send nae mair ! "
Said—" that cushion sae red, for my doggie's head,
   It is stuffed wi' thae locks o' hair."

" And didna ye get the letter, Ladye,
   Tied wi' a silken string,

The Lang Coortin'

Whilk I sent to thee frae the far countrie,
   A message of love to bring ? "

" It cam' to me frae the far countrie
   Wi' its silken string and a' ;
But it wasna prepaid," said that high-born maid,
   " Sae I gar'd them tak' it awa'."

" O ever alack that ye sent it back,
   It was written sae clerkly and well !
Now the message it brought, and the boon that it
      sought,
   I must even say it mysel'."

Then up and spake the popinjay,
   Sae wisely counselled he.
" Now say it in the proper way :
   Gae doon upon thy knee ! "

The lover he turned baith red and pale,
   Went doon upon his knee :
" O Ladye, hear the waesome tale
   That must be told to thee !

" For five lang years, and five lang years,
   I coorted thee by looks ;
By nods and winks, by smiles and tears,
   As I had read in books.

" For ten lang years, O weary hours !
   I coorted thee by signs ;
By sending game, by sending flowers,
   By sending Valentines.

The Lang Coortin'

" For five lang years, and five lang years,
   I have dwelt in the far countrie,
Till that thy mind should be inclined
   Mair tenderly to me.

" Now thirty years are gane and past,
   I am come frae a foreign land :
I am come to tell thee my love at last—
   O Ladye, gie me thy hand ! "

The ladye she turned not pale nor red,
   But she smiled a pitiful smile :
" Sic' a coortin' as yours, my man," she said,
   " Takes a lang and a weary while ! "

And out and laughed the popinjay,
   A laugh of bitter scorn :
" A coortin' done in sic' a way,
   It ought not to be borne ! "

Wi' that the doggie barked aloud,
   And up and doon he ran,
And tugged and strained his chain o' gowd,
   All for to bite the man.

" O hush thee, gentle popinjay !
   O hush thee, doggie dear !
There is a word I fain wad say,
   It needeth he should hear ! "

Aye louder screamed that ladye fair
   To drown her doggie's bark :
Ever the lover shouted mair
   To make that ladye hark :

"AND OUT AND LAUGHED THE POPINJAY"

The Lang Coortin'

Shrill and more shrill the popinjay
    Upraised his angry squall :
I trow the doggie's voice that day
    Was louder than them all !

The serving-men and serving-maids
    Sat by the kitchen fire :
They heard sic' a din the parlour within
    As made them much admire.

Out spake the boy in buttons
    (I ween he wasna thin),
" Now wha will tae the parlour gae,
    And stay this deadlie din ? "

And they have taen a kerchief,
    Casted their kevils in,
For wha will tae the parlour gae,
    And stay that deadlie din.

When on that boy the kevil fell
    To stay the fearsome noise,
" Gae in," they cried, " whate'er betide,
    Thou prince of button-boys ! "

Syne, he has taen a supple cane
    To swinge that dog sae fat :
The doggie yowled, the doggie howled
    The louder aye for that.

Syne, he has taen a mutton-bane—
    The doggie ceased his noise,
And followed doon the kitchen stair
    That prince of button-boys !

"THE DOGGIE CEASED HIS NOISE"

The Lang Coortin'

Then sadly spake that ladye fair,
  Wi' a frown upon her brow :
" O dearer to me is my sma' doggie
  Than a dozen sic' as thou !

" Nae use, nae use for sighs and tears :
  Nae use at all to fret :
Sin' ye've bided sae well for thirty years,
  Ye may bide a wee langer yet ! "

Sadly, sadly he crossed the floor
  And tirlëd at the pin :
Sadly went he through the door
  Where sadly he cam' in.

The Lang Coortin'

" O gin I had a popinjay
  To fly abune my head,
To tell me what I ought to say,
  I had by this been wed.

" O gin I find anither ladye,"
  He said wi' sighs and tears,
" I wot my coortin' sall not be
  Anither thirty years

" For gin I find a ladye gay,
  Exactly to my taste,
I'll pop the question, aye or nay,
  In twenty years at maist."

FOUR RIDDLES

[These consist of two Double Acrostics and two Charades.

No. I. was written at the request of some young friends, who had gone to a ball at an Oxford Commemoration—and also as a specimen of what might be done by making the Double Acrostic *a connected poem* instead of what it has hitherto been, a string of disjointed stanzas, on every conceivable subject, and about as interesting to read straight through as a page of a Cyclopædia. The first two stanzas describe the two main words, and each subsequent stanza one of the cross " lights."

No. II. was written after seeing Miss Ellen Terry perform in the play of " Hamlet." In this case the first stanza describes the two main words.

No. III. was written after seeing Miss Marion Terry perform in Mr. Gilbert's play of " Pygmalion and Galatea." The three stanzas respectively describe " My First," " My Second," and " My Whole."]

I

THERE was an ancient City, stricken down
  With a strange frenzy, and for many a day
They paced from morn to eve the crowded town,
    And danced the night away.

Four Riddles

I asked the cause : the aged man grew sad :
  They pointed to a building gray and tall,
And hoarsely answered " Step inside, my lad,
    And then you'll see it all."

Yet what are all such gaieties to me
  Whose thoughts are full of indices and surds ?

$$x^2 + 7x + 53 = \frac{11}{3}.$$

But something whispered " It will soon be done :
  Bands cannot always play, nor ladies smile :
Endure with patience the distasteful fun
    For just a little while ! "

A change came o'er my Vision—it was night :
  We clove a pathway through a frantic throng :
The steeds, wild-plunging, filled us with affright :
    The chariots whirled along.

Within a marble hall a river ran—
  A living tide, half muslin and half cloth :
And here one mourned a broken wreath or fan,
    Yet swallowed down her wrath ;

And here one offered to a thirsty fair
  (His words half-drowned amid those thunders
  tuneful)
Some frozen viand (there were many there),
    A tooth-ache in each spoonful.

There comes a happy pause, for human strength
  Will not endure to dance without cessation ;

Four Riddles

And every one must reach the point at length
      Of absolute prostration.

At such a moment ladies learn to give,
  To partners who would urge them overmuch,
A flat and yet decided negative—
      Photographers love such.

There comes a welcome summons—hope revives,
  And fading eyes grow bright, and pulses quicken :
Incessant pop the corks, and busy knives
      Dispense the tongue and chicken.

Flushed with new life, the crowd flows back again :
  And all is tangled talk and mazy motion—
Much like a waving field of golden grain,
      Or a tempestuous ocean.

And thus they give the time, that Nature meant
  For peaceful sleep and meditative snores,
To ceaseless din and mindless merriment
      And waste of shoes and floors.

And One (we name him not) that flies the flowers,
  That dreads the dances, and that shuns the salads,
They doom to pass in solitude the hours,
      Writing acrostic-ballads.

How late it grows !   The hour is surely past
  That should have warned us with its double knock ?
The twilight wanes, and morning comes at last—
      " Oh, Uncle, what's o'clock ? "

The Uncle gravely nods, and wisely winks.
  It *may* mean much, but how is one to know ?

Four Riddles

He opes his mouth—yet out of it, methinks,
 No words of wisdom flow.

Answer : Commemoration, Monstrosities.

II

EMPRESS of Art, for thee I twine
 This wreath with all too slender skill.
Forgive my Muse each halting line,
 And for the deed accept the will !

O day of tears ! Whence comes this spectre grim,
 Parting, like Death's cold river, souls that love ?
Is not he bound to thee, as thou to him,
 By vows, unwhispered here, yet heard above ?

And still it lives, that keen and heavenward flame,
 Lives in his eye, and trembles in his tone :
And these wild words of fury but proclaim
 A heart that beats for thee, for thee alone !

But all is lost : that mighty mind o'erthrown,
 Like sweet bells jangled, piteous sight to see !
" Doubt that the stars are fire," so runs his moan,
 " Doubt Truth herself, but not my love for thee ! "

A sadder vision yet : thine aged sire
 Shaming his hoary locks with treacherous wile !
And dost thou now doubt Truth to be a liar ?
 And wilt thou die, that hast forgot to smile ?

Nay, get thee hence ! Leave all thy winsome ways
 And the faint fragrance of thy scattered flowers :
In holy silence wait the appointed days,
 And weep away the leaden-footed hours.

Answer : Ellen Terry.

Four Riddles

III

THE air is bright with hues of light
  And rich with laughter and with singing :
Young hearts beat high in ecstasy,
  And banners wave, and bells are ringing :
But silence falls with fading day,
And there's an end to mirth and play.
        Ah, well-a-day !

Rest your old bones, ye wrinkled crones !
  The kettle sings, the firelight dances.
Deep be it quaffed, the magic draught
  That fills the soul with golden fancies !
For Youth and Pleasance will not stay,
And ye are withered, worn, and gray.
        Ah, well-a-day !

O fair cold face ! O form of grace,
  For human passion madly yearning !
O weary air of dumb despair,
  From marble won, to marble turning !
" Leave us not thus ! " we fondly pray.
" We cannot let thee pass away ! "
        Ah, well-a-day !
      Answer : Galatea (Gala-tea).

IV

MY First is singular at best :
    More plural is my Second :
My Third is far the pluralest—
So plural-plural, I protest
    It scarcely can be reckoned !

Four Riddles

My First is followed by a bird :
   My Second by believers
In magic art : my simple Third
Follows, too often, hopes absurd
   And plausible deceivers.

My First to get at wisdom tries—
   A failure melancholy !
My Second men revered as wise :
My Third from heights of wisdom flies
   To depths of frantic folly.

My First is ageing day by day :
   My Second's age is ended :
My Third enjoys an age, they say,
That never seems to fade away,
   Through centuries extended.

My Whole ?   I need a poet's pen
   To paint her myriad phases :
The monarch, and the slave, of men—
A mountain-summit, and a den
   Of dark and deadly mazes—

A flashing light—a fleeting shade—
   Beginning, end, and middle
Of all that human art hath made
Or wit devised ! Go, seek *her* aid,
   If you would read my riddle !

Answer : Imagination (I-Magi-nation).

FAME'S PENNY-TRUMPET

[Affectionately dedicated to all " original researchers "
who pant for " endowment."]

Blow, blow your trumpets till they crack,
  Ye little men of little souls !
And bid them huddle at your back—
  Gold-sucking leeches, shoals on shoals !

Fill all the air with hungry wails—
  " Reward us, ere we think or write !
Without your Gold mere Knowledge fails
  To sate the swinish appetite ! "

And, where great Plato paced serene,
  Or Newton paused with wistful eye,
Rush to the chace with hoofs unclean
  And Babel-clamour of the sty.

Be yours the pay : be theirs the praise :
  We will not rob them of their due,
Nor vex the ghosts of other days
  By naming them along with you.

They sought and found undying fame :
  They toiled not for reward nor thanks :
Their cheeks are hot with honest shame
  For you, the modern mountebanks !

Fame's Penny-Trumpet

Who preach of Justice—plead with tears
    That Love and Mercy should abound—
While marking with complacent ears
    The moaning of some tortured hound :

Who prate of Wisdom—nay, forbear,
    Lest Wisdom turn on you in wrath,
Trampling, with heel that will not spare,
    The vermin that beset her path !

Go, throng each other's drawing-rooms,
    Ye idols of a petty clique :
Strut your brief hour in borrowed plumes,
    And make your penny-trumpets squeak :

Deck your dull talk with pilfered shreds
    Of learning from a nobler time,
And oil each other's little heads
    With mutual Flattery's golden slime :

And when the topmost height ye gain,
    And stand in Glory's ether clear,
And grasp the prize of all your pain—
    So many hundred pounds a year—

Then let Fame's banner be unfurled !
    Sing Pæans for a victory won !
Ye tapers, that would light the world,
    And cast a shadow on the Sun—

Who still shall pour His rays sublime,
    One crystal flood, from East to West,
When *ye* have burned your little time
    And feebly flickered into rest !

FROM

COLLEGE RHYMES

ODE TO DAMON

(From Chloë, who Understands His Meaning.)

" Oh, do not forget the day when we met
　At the fruiterer's shop in the city :
When you *said* I was plain and *excessively* vain,
　But I knew that you *meant* I was pretty.

" Recollect, too, the hour when I purchased the flour
　(For the dumplings, you know) and the suet ;
Whilst the apples I told my dear Damon to hold,
　(Just to see if you knew how to do it).

" Then recall to your mind how you left *me* behind,
　And went off in a 'bus with the pippins ;
When you *said* you'd forgot, but I knew you had *not* ;
　(It was merely to save the odd threepence !).

" Don't forget your delight in the dumplings that night,
　Though you *said* they were tasteless and doughy :
But you winked as you spoke, and I saw that the joke
　(*If it was one*) was meant for your Chloë !

Ode to Damon

" Then remember the day when Joe offered to pay
    For us all at the Great Exhibition ;
You proposed a short cut, and we found the thing
        shut,
    (We were two hours too late for admission).

" Your ' short cut ', dear, we found took us *seven miles
        round*
    (And Joe said exactly what *we* did) :
Well, *I* helped you out then—it was just like you men—
    Not an atom of sense when it's needed !

" *You* said ' What's to be done ? ' and *I* thought you
        in fun,
    (Never *dreaming* you were such a ninny).
' *Home* directly ! ' said I, and you paid for the fly,
    (And I *think* that you gave him a guinea).

" Well, *that* notion, you said, had not entered your
        head :
    You proposed ' The best thing, as we're come, is
(Since it opens again in the morning at ten)
    To wait '—*Oh, you prince of all dummies !*

" And when Joe asked you ' Why, if a man were to die,
    Just as you ran a sword through his middle,
You'd be hung for the crime ? ' and you said ' Give me
        time ! '
    And brought to your Chloë the riddle—

" Why, remember, you dunce, how I solved it at once—
    (The question which Joe had referred to you),
Why, I told you the cause, was ' the force of the laws,'
    And you said ' *It had never occurred to you.*'

Ode to Damon

" This instance will show that your brain is too slow,
    And (though your exterior is showy),
Yet so arrant a goose can be no sort of use
    To society—come to your Chloë !

" You'll find *no one* like me, who can manage to see
    Your meaning, you talk so obscurely :
Why, if once I were gone, how *would* you get on ?
    Come, you know what I mean, Damon, surely."

1861.

THOSE HORRID HURDY-GURDIES!

A Monody, by a Victim

" My mother bids me bind my hair,"
  And not go about such a figure ;
It's a bother, of course, but what do I care ?
  I shall do as I please when I'm bigger.

" My lodging is on the cold, cold ground,"
  As the first-floor and attic were taken.
I tried the garret but once, and found
  That my wish for a change was mistaken.

" Ever of thee ! " yes, " Ever of thee ! "
  They chatter more and more,
Till I groan aloud, " Oh ! let me be !
  I have heard it all before ! "

" Please remember the organ, sir,"
  What ? hasn't he left me yet ?
I promise, good man ; for its tedious burr
  I never can forget.

1861.

MY FANCY

I PAINTED her a gushing thing,
  With years perhaps a score ;
I little thought to find they were
  At least a dozen more ;
My fancy gave her eyes of blue,
  A curly auburn head :
I came to find the blue a green,
  The auburn turned to red.

She boxed my ears this morning,
  They tingled very much ;
I own that I could wish her
  A somewhat lighter touch ;
And if you were to ask me how
  Her charms might be improved,
I would not have them *added to*,
  But just a few *removed* !

She has the bear's ethereal grace,
  The bland hyena's laugh,
The footstep of the elephant,
  The neck of the giraffe ;
I love her still, believe me,
  Though my heart its passion hides ;
" She 's all my fancy painted her,"
  But oh ! *how much besides !*

Mar. 15, 1862.

THE MAJESTY OF JUSTICE

AN OXFORD IDYLL

THEY passed beneath the College gate ;
  And down the High went slowly on ;
Then spake the Undergraduate
  To that benign and portly Don :
" They say that Justice is a Queen—
  A Queen of awful Majesty—
Yet in the papers I have seen
  Some things that puzzle me.

" A Court obscure, so rumour states,
  There is, called ' Vice-Cancellarii,'
Which keeps on Undergraduates,
  Who do not pay their bills, a wary eye.
A case I'm told was lately brought
  Into that tiniest of places,
And justice in that case was sought—
  As in most other cases.

" Well ! Justice as I hold, dear friend,
  Is Justice, neither more than less :
I never dreamed it could depend
  On ceremonial or dress.

The Majesty of Justice

I thought that her imperial sway
  In Oxford surely would appear,
But all the papers seem to say
  She 's not majestic *here*."

The portly Don he made reply,
  With the most roguish of his glances,
" Perhaps she drops her Majesty
  Under peculiar circumstances."
" But that's the point ! " the young man cried,
  " The puzzle that I wish to pen you in—
How are the public to decide
  Which article is genuine ?

" Is't only when the Court is large
  That we for ' Majesty ' need hunt ?
Would what is Justice in a barge
  Be something different in a punt ? "
" Nay, nay ! " the Don replied, amused,
  " You're talking nonsense, sir ! You know it !
Such arguments were never used
  By any friend of Jowett."

" Then is it in the men who trudge
  (Beef-eaters I believe they call them)
Before each wigged and ermined judge,
  For fear some mischief should befall them ?
If I should recognise in one
  (Through all disguise) my own domestic,
I fear 'twould shed a gleam of fun
  Even on the ' Majestic ' ! "

The Majesty of Justice

The portly Don replied, " Ahem !
   They can't exactly be its *essence* :
I scarcely think the want of them
   The ' Majesty of Justice ' lessens.
Besides, they always march awry ;
   Their gorgeous garments never fit :
Processions don't make Majesty—
   I'm quite convinced of it."

" Then is it in the *wig* it lies,
   Whose countless rows of rigid curls
Are gazed at with admiring eyes
   By country lads and servant-girls ? "
Out laughed that bland and courteous Don :
   " Dear sir, I do not mean to flatter—
But surely you have hit upon
   The essence of the matter.

" They will not own the Majesty
   Of Justice, making Monarchs bow,
Unless as evidence they see
   The horsehair wig upon her brow.
Yes, yes ! That makes the silliest men
   Seem wise ; the meanest men look big :
The Majesty of Justice, then,
   Is seated in the WIG."

March 1863.

240

FROM

NOTES BY AN OXFORD CHIEL

THE ELECTIONS TO THE HEBDOMADAL COUNCIL

[In the year 1866, a Letter with the above title was published in Oxford, addressed by Mr. Goldwin Smith to the Senior Censor of Christ Church, with the two-fold object of revealing to the University a vast political misfortune which it had unwittingly encountered, and of suggesting a remedy which should at once alleviate the bitterness of the calamity and secure the sufferers from its recurrence. The misfortune thus revealed was no less than the fact that, at a recent election of Members to the Hebdomadal Council, *two* Conservatives had been chosen, thus giving a Conservative majority in the Council; and the remedy suggested was a sufficiently sweeping one, embracing, as it did, the following details :—

1. " The exclusion " (from Congregation) " of the non-academical elements which form a main part of the strength of this party domination." These " elements " are afterwards enumerated as " the parish clergy and the professional men of the city, and chaplains who are without any academical occupation."

2. The abolition of the Hebdomadal Council.

3. The abolition of the legislative functions of Convocation.

These are all the main features of this remarkable scheme of Reform, unless it be necessary to add—

4. " To preside over a Congregation with full legislative powers, the Vice-Chancellor ought no doubt to be a man of real capacity."

But it would be invidious to suppose that there was any intention of suggesting this as a novelty.

The following rhythmical version of the Letter develops its principles to an extent which possibly the writer had never contemplated.]

" *Now is the winter of our discontent.*" [1]

" HEARD ye the arrow hurtle in the sky ?
Heard ye the dragon-monster's deathful cry ? "—
Excuse this sudden burst of the Heroic ;
The present state of things would vex a Stoic !
And just as Sairey Gamp, for pains within,
Administered a modicum of gin,
So does my mind, when vexed and ill at ease,
Console itself with soothing similes,
The " dragon-monster " (pestilential schism !)
I need not tell you is Conservatism ;
The " hurtling arrow " (till we find a better)
Is represented by the present Letter.
    'Twas, I remember, but the other day,
Dear Senior Censor, that you chanced to say
You thought these party-combinations would
Be found, " though needful, no unmingled good."

[1] Dr. Wynter, President of St. John's, one of the recently elected Conservative members of Council.

The Elections to the Hebdomadal Council

Unmingled good ?   They are unmingled ill ! [1]
I never took to them, and never will—— [2]
What am I saying ?   Heed it not, my friend :
On the next page I mean to recommend
The very dodges that I now condemn
In the Conservatives !   Don't hint to them
A word of this !   (In confidence.   Ahem !)
   Need I rehearse the history of Jowett ?
I need not, Senior Censor, for you know it. [3]
That was the Board Hebdomadal, and oh !
Who would be free, themselves must strike the blow !
Let each that wears a beard, and each that shaves,
Join in the cry " We never will be slaves ! "
" But can the University afford
To be a slave to any kind of board ?
A *slave ?* " you shuddering ask.   " Think you it can,
     Sir ? "
" *Not at the present moment,*" is my answer. [4]
I've thought the matter o'er and o'er again
And given to it all my powers of brain ;
I've thought it out, and this is what I make it,
(And I don't care a Tory how you take it :)
It may be right to go ahead, I guess:
It may be right to stop, I do confess ;
Also, it may be right to retrogress. [5]

---

[1] " In a letter on a point connected with the late elections to the Hebdomadal Council you incidentally remarked to me that our combinations for these elections, ' though necessary were not an unmixed good.' They are an unmixed evil."

[2] " I never go to a *caucus* without reluctance : I never write a canvassing letter without a feeling of repugnance to my task."

[3] " I need not rehearse the history of the Regius Professor of Greek."

[4] " The University cannot afford at the present moment to be delivered over as a slave to any non-academical interest whatever."

[5] " It may be right to go on, it may be right to stand still, or it may be right to go back."

The Elections to the Hebdomadal Council

So says the oracle, and, for myself, I
Must say it beats to fits the one at Delphi !
  To save beloved Oxford from the yoke,
(For this majority's beyond a joke),
We must combine,[1] aye ! hold a *caucus*-meeting,[2]
Unless we want to get another beating.
That they should " bott!e " us is nothing new—
But shall they bottle us and *caucus* too ?
See the " fell unity of purpose " now
With which Obstructives plunge into the row ![3]
" Factious Minorities," we used to sigh—
" Factious Majorities ! " is now the cry.
" Votes—ninety-two "—no combination here :
" Votes—ninety-three "—conspiracy, 'tis clear ![4]
You urge " 'Tis but a unit."   I reply
That in that unit lurks their " unity."
Our voters often bolt, and often baulk us,
But then, they never, never go *to caucus !*
Our voters can't forget the maxim famous
  " *Semel electum semper eligamus* " :
They never can be worked into a ferment
By visionary promise of preferment,
Nor taught, by hints of " Paradise "[5] beguiled,

[1] " To save the University from going completely under the yoke . . . we shall still be obliged to combine."
[2] " Caucus-holding and wire-pulling would still be almost inevitably carried on to some extent."
[3] " But what are we to do ? Here is a great political and theological party . . . labouring under perfect discipline and with fell unity of purpose, to hold the University in subjection, and fill her government with its nominees."
[4] At a recent election to Council, the Liberals mustered ninety-two votes and the Conservatives ninety-three ; whereupon the latter were charged with having obtained their victory by a conspiracy.
[5] Not to mention that, as we cannot promise Paradise to our supporters, they are very apt to take the train for London just before the election.

The Elections to the Hebdomadal Council

To whisper " C for Chairman " like a child ! [1]
And thus the friends that we have tempted down
Oft take the two-o'clock Express for town.[2]
   This is our danger : this the secret foe
That aims at Oxford such a deadly blow.
What champion can we find to save the State,
To crush the plot ? We darkly whisper " Wait ! " [3]
   My scheme is this : remove the votes of all
The residents that are not Liberal—[4]
Leave the young Tutors uncontrolled and free,
And Oxford then shall see—what it shall see.
What next ? Why then, I say, let Convocation
Be shorn of all her powers of legislation.[5]
But why stop there ? Let us go boldly on—
Sweep everything beginning with a " Con "
Into oblivion ! Convocation first,
Conservatism next, and, last and worst,
   " *Concilium Hebdomadale* " must,
Consumed and conquered, be consigned to dust ! [6]

[1] It is not known to what the word " Paradise " was intended to allude, and therefore the hint, here thrown out, that the writer meant to recall the case of the late Chairman of Mr. Gladstone's committee, who had been recently collated to the See of Chester, is wholly wanton and gratuitous.

[2] A case of this kind had actually occurred on the occasion of the division just alluded to.

[3] Mr. Wayte, now President of Trinity, then put forward as the Liberal candidate for election to Council.

[4] " You and others suggest, as the only effective remedy, that the Constituency should be reformed, by the exclusion of the non-academical elements which form a main part of the strength of this party domination."

[5] " I confess that, having included all the really academical elements in Congregation, I would go boldly on, and put an end to the Legislative functions of Convocation."

[6] " This conviction, that while we have Elections to Council we shall not entirely get rid of party organisation and its evils, leads me to venture a step further, and to raise the question whether it is really necessary that we should have an Elective Council for legislative purposes at all."

The Elections to the Hebdomadal Council

And here I must relate a little fable
I heard last Saturday at our high table :—
The cats, it seems, were masters of the house,
And held their own against the rat and mouse :
Of course the others couldn't stand it long,
So held a caucus (not, in their case, wrong) ;
And, when they were assembled to a man,
Uprose an aged rat, and thus began :—
   " Brothers in bondage !   Shall we bear to be
For ever left in a minority ?
With what ' fell unity of purpose ' cats
Oppose the trusting innocence of rats !
So unsuspicious are we of disguise,
Their machinations take us by surprise—[1]
Insulting and tyrannical absurdities ! [2]
It is too bad by half—upon my word it is !
For, now that these Con——, cats, I should say (frizzle
         'em !),
Are masters, they exterminate like Islam ! [3]
How shall we deal with them ?   I'll tell you how :—
Let none but kittens be allowed to miaow !
The Liberal kittens seize us but in play,
And, while they frolic, we can run away :
But older cats are not so generous,
Their claws are too Conservative for us !
Then let *them* keep the stable and the oats,
While kittens, rats, and mice have all the votes.
   " Yes ; banish cats !   The kittens would not use
Their powers for blind obstruction,[4] nor refuse

[1] " Sometimes, indeed, not being informed that the wires are at work, we are completely taken by surprise."
[2] " We are without protection against this most insulting and tyrannical absurdity."   [3] " It is as exterminating as Islam."
[4] " Their powers would scarcely be exercised for the purposes of fanaticism, or in a spirit of blind obstruction."

The Elections to the Hebdomadal Council

To let us sip the cream and gnaw the cheese—
How glorious then would be our destinies ! [1]
Kittens and rats would occupy the throne,
And rule the larder for itself alone ! " [2]
    So rhymed my friend, and asked me what I thought
of it.
I told him that so much as I had caught of it
Appeared to me (as I need hardly mention)
Entirely undeserving of attention.
    But now, to guide the Congregation, when
It numbers none but really " able " men,
A " *Vice-Cancellarius* " will be needed
Of every kind of human weakness weeded !
Is such the president that we have got ?
He ought no doubt to be ; why should he not ? [3]
I do not hint that Liberals should dare
To oust the present holder of the chair—
But surely he would not object to be
Gently examined by a Board of three ?
Their duty being just to ascertain
That he's " all there " (I mean, of course, in brain),
And that his mind, from " petty details " clear,
Is fitted for the duties of his sphere.
    All this is merely moonshine, till we get
The seal of Parliament upon it set.

---

[1] " These narrow local bounds, within which our thoughts and schemes have hitherto been pent, will begin to disappear, and a far wider sphere of action will open on the view."
[2] " Those councils must be freely opened to all who can serve her well and who will serve her for herself."
[3] " To preside over a Congregation with full legislative powers, the Vice-Chancellor ought no doubt to be a man of real capacity; but why should he not ? His mind ought also, for this as well as for his other high functions, to be clear of petty details, and devoted to the great matters of University business; but why should not this condition also be fulfilled ? "

A word then, Senior Censor, in your ear :
The Government is in a state of fear—
Like some old gentleman, abroad at night,
Seized with a sudden shiver of affright,
Who offers money, on his bended knees,
To the first skulking vagabond he sees—
Now is the lucky moment for our task ;
They daren't refuse us anything we ask ![1]

And then our Fellowships shall open be
To Intellect, no meaner quality !
No moral excellence, no social fitness
Shall ever be admissible as witness.
" Avaunt, dull Virtue ! " is Oxonia's cry :
" Come to my arms, ingenious Villainy ! "

For Classic Fellowships, an honour high,
Simonides and Co. will then apply—
Our Mathematics will to Oxford bring
The 'cutest members of the betting-ring—
Law Fellowships will start upon their journeys
A myriad of unscrupulous attorneys—
While prisoners, doomed till now to toil unknown,
Shall mount the Physical Professor's throne !
And thus would Oxford educate, indeed,
Men far beyond a merely local need—
With no career before them, I may say,[2]
Unless they're wise enough to go away,

[1] " If you apply now to Parliament for this or any other University reform, you will find the House of Commons in a propitious mood. . . . Even the Conservative Government, as it looks for the support of moderate Liberals on the one great subject, is very unwilling to present itself in such an aspect that these men may not be able decently to give it their support."

[2] " With open Fellowships, Oxford will soon produce a supply of men fit for the work of high education far beyond her own local demands, and in fact with no career before them unless a career can be opened elsewhere."

The Elections to the Hebdomadal Council

And seek far West, or in the distant East,
Another flock of pigeons to be fleeced.

    I might go on, and trace the destiny
Of Oxford in an age which, though it be
Thus breaking with tradition, owns a new
Allegiance to the intellectual few—
(I mean, of course, the—pshaw ! no matter who !)
But, were I to pursue the boundless theme,
I fear that I should seem to you to dream.[1]

    This to fulfil, or even—humbler far—
To shun Conservatism's noxious star
And all the evils that it brings behind,
These pestilential coils must be untwined—
The party-coils, that clog the march of Mind—
Choked in whose meshes Oxford, slowly wise,
Has lain for three disastrous centuries.[2]
Away with them! (It is for this I yearn !)
Each twist untwist, each Turner overturn !
Disfranchise each Conservative, and cancel
The votes of Michell, Liddon, Wall, and Mansel !
Then, then shall Oxford be herself again,
Neglect the heart, and cultivate the brain—
Then this shall be the burden of our song,
" All change is good—whatever is, is wrong—"
Then Intellect's proud flag shall be unfurled,
And Brain, and Brain alone, shall rule the world !

[1] " I should seem to you to dream if I were to say what I think
the destiny of the University may be in an age which, though it is
breaking with tradition, is, from the same causes, owning a new
allegiance to intellectual authority."

[2] " But to fulfil this, or even a far humbler destiny—to escape
the opposite lot—the pestilential coils of party, in which the
University has lain for three disastrous centuries choked, must be
untwined."

THE DESERTED PARKS

(On the proposal that portions of the University Parks should
be turned into cricket-grounds and allotted to cricket-clubs and
colleges.)

" Solitudinem faciunt : *Parcum* appellant."

MUSEUM ! loveliest building of the plain
Where Cherwell winds towards the distant main ;
How often have I loitered o'er thy green,
Where humble happiness endeared the scene !
How often have I paused on every charm,
The rustic couple walking arm in arm—
The groups of trees, with seats beneath the shade
For prattling babes and whisp'ring lovers made—
The never-failing brawl, the busy mill
Where tiny urchins vied in fistic skill—
(Two phrases only have that dusky race
Caught from the learned influence of the place ;
Phrases in their simplicity sublime,
" Scramble a copper ! " " Please, Sir, what's the
    time ? ")
These round thy walks their cheerful influence shed ;
These were thy charms—but all these charms are fled.
    Amidst thy bowers the tyrant's hand is seen,
And rude pavilions sadden all thy green ;

The Deserted Parks

One selfish pastime grasps the whole domain,
And half a faction swallows up the plain ;
Adown thy glades, all sacrificed to cricket,
The hollow-sounding bat now guards the wicket ;
Sunk are thy mounds in shapeless level all,
Lest aught impede the swiftly rolling ball ;
And trembling, shrinking from the fatal blow,
Far, far away thy hapless children go.

Ill fares the place, to luxury a prey,
Where wealth accumulates, and minds decay ;
Athletic sports may flourish or may fade,
Fashion may make them, even as it has made ;
But the broad parks, the city's joy and pride,
When once destroyed can never be supplied !

Ye friends to truth, ye statesmen, who survey
The rich man's joys increase, the poor's decay,
'Tis yours to judge, how wide the limits stand
Between a splendid and a happy land.
Proud swells go by with laugh of hollow joy,
And shouting Folly hails them with " Ahoy ! "
Funds even beyond the miser's wish abound,
And rich men flock from all the world around.
Yet count our gains. This wealth is but a name,
That leaves our useful products still the same.
Not so the loss. The man of wealth and pride
Takes up a space that many poor supplied ;
Space for the game, and all its instruments,
Space for pavilions and for scorers' tents ;
The ball, that raps his shins in padding cased,
Has worn the verdure to an arid waste ;
His Park, where these exclusive sports are seen,
Indignant spurns the rustic from the green ;
While through the plain, consigned to silence all,

251

The Deserted Parks

In barren splendour flits the russet ball.
  In peaceful converse with his brother Don,
Here oft the calm Professor wandered on ;
Strange words he used—men drank with wondering
    ears
The languages called " dead," the tongues of other
    years.
(Enough of Heber ! Let me once again
Attune my verse to Goldsmith's liquid strain.)
A man he was to undergraduates dear,
And passing rich with forty pounds a year.
And so, I ween, he would have been till now,
Had not his friends ('twere long to tell you how)
Prevailed on him, Jack-Horner-like, to try
Some method to evaluate his pie,
And win from those dark depths, with skilful thumb,
Five times a hundredweight of luscious plum—
Yet for no thirst of wealth, no love of praise,
In learned labour he consumed his days !

  O Luxury ! thou cursed by Heaven's decree,
How ill exchanged are things like these for thee !
How do thy potions, with insidious joy,
Diffuse their pleasures only to destroy ;
Iced cobbler, Badminton, and shandy-gaff,
Rouse the loud jest and idiotic laugh ;
Inspired by them, to tipsy greatness grown,
Men boast a florid vigour not their own ;
At every draught more wild and wild they grow ;
While pitying friends observe " I told you so ! "
Till, summoned to their post, at the first ball,
A feeble under-hand, their wickets fall.

  Even now the devastation is begun,
And half the business of destruction done ;

The Deserted Parks

Even now, methinks while pondering here in pity,
I see the rural Virtues leave the city.
Contented Toil, and calm scholastic Care,
And frugal Moderation, all are there ;
Resolute Industry that scorns the lure
Of careless mirth—that dwells apart secure—
To science gives her days, her midnight oil,
Cheered by the sympathy of others' toil—
Courtly Refinement, and that Taste in dress
That brooks no meanness, yet avoids excess—
All these I see, with slow reluctant pace
Desert the long-beloved and honoured place !

   While yet 'tis time, Oxonia, rise and fling
The spoiler from thee : grant no parleying !
Teach him that eloquence, against the wrong,
Though very poor, may still be very strong ;
That party-interests we must forgo,
When hostile to " pro bono publico " ;
That faction's empire hastens to its end,
When once mankind to common sense attend ;
While independent votes may win the day
Even against the potent spell of " Play ! "

May 1867.

THE NEW BELFRY OF CHRIST
CHURCH, OXFORD

East view of the new Belfry, Ch. Ch., as seen from the Meadow.

[" In or about the year 1871, one of the old canons' houses, which stood between the cathedral and the ' Tom ' Quadrangle, was vacated, and the authorities agreed that it should be demolished, in order to make space for a direct approach to the cathedral from the quadrangle. Dean Liddell called in the aid of Mr. Bodley, who constructed a double archway, running under the solid masonry, and of sufficient length to warrant the critics in describing it as the Tunnel. About the same time it was decided to remove the bells from the tower of the cathedral, and make a new belfry over the staircase of the Hall. The arcade of the tower was cut through for the purpose of liberating the bells, and the gap in the stonework is referred to by Mr. Dodgson as the Trench. From lack of funds, or some other reason, Bodley's idea of a campanile of wood and copper was not proceeded with, and the bells were ensconced in a plain wooden case, of which the author of The New Belfry '—first printed in 1872, and hurried by the Oxford public through five editions—made merciless fun. He likens it to a meat-safe, a box, a Greek Lexicon, a parallelepiped, a bathing-machine, a piece of bar soap, a tea-caddy, a clothes-horse; but his favourite name for it is the Tea-chest. The Tunnel, the Trench, and the Tea-chest are the ' three T's.' "
—Collingwood's *Lewis Carroll Picture-Book.*]

254

The New Belfry of Christ Church, Oxford

IF thou wouldst view the Belfry aright,
Go visit it at the mirk midnight—
For the least hint of open day
Scares the beholder quite away.
When wall and window are black as pitch,
And there's no deciding which is which;
When the dark Hall's uncertain roof
In horror seems to stand aloof;
When corner and corner, alternately,
Is wrought to an odious symmetry:
When distant Thames is heard to sigh
And shudder as he hurries by;
Then go, if it be worth the while,
Then view the Belfry's monstrous pile,
And, home returning, soothly swear,
    " 'Tis more than Job himself could bear ! "

*On the feelings with which resident Ch. Ch. men regard
the new Belfry.*

Is it the glow of conscious pride—
Of pure ambition gratified—
That seeks to read in other eye
Something of its own ecstasy ?
Or wrath, that worldlings should make fun
Of anything " the House " has done ?
Or puzzlement, that seeks in vain
The rigid mystery to explain ?
Or is it shame that, knowing not
How to defend or cloak the blot—
The foulest blot on fairest face
That ever marred a noble place—
Burns with the pangs it will not own,
Pangs felt by loyal sons alone ?

255

The New Belfry of Christ Church, Oxford

Song and Chorus.

Five fathom square the Belfry frowns ;
   All its sides of timber made ;
Painted all in grays and browns ;
   Nothing of it that will fade.
Christ Church may admire the change—
Oxford thinks it sad and strange.
Beauty's dead !   Let's ring her knell.
Hark ! now I hear them—ding-dong, bell.

On the moral of the new Belfry.

" Look on the Quadrangle of Christ, squarely, for is it
   not a Square ?
And a Square recalleth a Cube ; and a Cube recalleth
   the Belfry ;
And the Belfry recalleth a Die, shaken by the hand of
   the gambler ;
Yet, once thrown, it may not be recalled, being, so to
   speak, irrevocable.
There it shall endure for ages, treading hard on the
   heels of the Sublime—
For it is but a step, saith the wise man, from the
   Sublime unto the Ridiculous :
And the Simple dwelleth midway between, and
   shareth the qualities of either."

THE WANDERING BURGESS

(" Our Willie " was Mr. Gladstone, who had been defeated at
Oxford in 1865, and had since represented South Lancashire and
Greenwich.)

Our Willie had been sae lang awa',
    Frae bonnie Oxford toon,
The townsfolk they were greeting a'
    As they went up and doon.

He hadna been gane a year, a year,
    A year but barely ten,
When word cam unto Oxford toon,
    Our Willie wad come agen.

Willie he stude at Thomas his Gate,
    And made a lustie din ;
And who so blithe as the gate-porter
    To rise and let him in ?

" Now enter, Willie, now enter, Willie,
    And look around the place,
And see the pain that we have ta'en
    Thomas his Quad to grace."

The first look that our Willie cast,
    He leuch loud laughters three,

The Wandering Burgess

The neist look that our Willie cast,
   The tear blindit his e'e.

Sae square and stark the Tea-chest frowned
   Athwart the upper air,
But when the Trench our Willie saw,
   He thoucht the Tea-chest fair.

Sae murderous-deep the Trench did gape
   The parapet aboon,
But when the Tunnel Willie saw,
   He loved the Trench eftsoon.

West view of the new Tunnel.

'Twas mirk beneath the tane archway,
   'Twas mirk beneath the tither ;
Ye wadna ken a man therein,
   Though it were your ain dear brither.

He turned him round and round about,
   And looked upon the Three ;
And dismal grew his countenance,
   And drumlie grew his e'e.

" What cheer, what cheer, my gallant knight ? "
   The gate-porter 'gan say.
" Saw ever ye sae fair a sight
   As ye have seen this day ? "

The Wandering Burgess

" Now haud your tongue of your prating, man :
　Of your prating now let me be.
For, as I'm true knight, a fouler sight
　I'll never live to see.

" Before I'd be the ruffian dark
　Who planned this ghastly show,
I'd serve as secretary's clerk
　To Ayrton or to Lowe.

" Before I'd own the loathly thing
　That Christ Church Quad reveals,
I'd serve as shoeblack's underling
　To Odger and to Beales ! "

A BACHANALIAN ODE

HERE'S to the Freshman of bashful eighteen !
   Here's to the Senior of twenty !
Here's to the youth whose moustache can't be seen !
   And here's to the man who has plenty !
      Let the man Pass !
      Out of the mass
I'll warrant we'll find you some fit for a Class !

Here's to the Censors, who symbolise Sense,
   Just as Mitres incorporate Might, Sir !
To the Bursar, who never expands the expense,
   And the Readers, who always do right, Sir.
      Tutor and Don,
      Let them job on !
I warrant they'll rival the centuries gone !

Here's to the Chapter, melodious crew !
   Whose harmony surely *intends* well :
For, though it commences with " harm," it is true,
   Yet its motto is " All's well that ends well ! "
      'Tis love, I'll be bound,
      That makes it go round !
For " In for a penny is in for a pound ! "

A Bachanalian Ode

Here's to the Governing Body, whose Art
  (For they're Masters of Arts to a man, Sir !)
Seeks to beautify Christ Church in every part,
    Though the method seems hardly to answer !
        With three T's it is graced—
        Which letters are placed
To stand for the names of Tact, Talent, and Taste !

EXAMINATION STATUTE

[" The Statute proposed to allow candidates for a degree to forsake Classics after Moderations, except so far as was needed for a Fourth Class in the Final School of Literæ Humaniores, if they wished to graduate in science. This Dodgson considered degrading both to Classics and to Mathematics."—*Dodgson Handbook.*]

A list of those who might, could, would, or should have voted thereon in Congregation, February 2, 4681, arranged alphabetically.

A is for [Acland], who'd physic the Masses,
B is for [Brodie], who swears by the gases.
C is for [Conington], constant to Horace.
D is for [Donkin], who integrates for us.
E is for [Evans], with rifle well steadied.
F is for [Freeman], Examiner dreaded !
G's [Goldwin Smith], by the " Saturday " quoted,
H is for [Heurtley], to " Margaret " devoted.
I am the Author, a rhymer erratic—
J is for [Jowett], who lectures in Attic :
K is for [Kitchen], than attic much warmer.
L is for [Liddell], relentless reformer !
M is for [Mansel], our Logic-provider,
And [Norris] is N, once a famous rough-rider.
[Ogilvie]'s O, Orthodoxy's Mendoza !
And [Parker] is P, the amendment-proposer.
Q is the Quad, where the Dons are collecting.
R is for [Rolleston], who lives for dissecting :

262

Examination Statute

S is for [Stanley], sworn foe to formality.
T's [Travers Twiss], full of civil legality.
U's University, factiously splitting—
V's the Vice-Chancellor, ceaselessly sitting.
W's [Wall], by Museum made frantic,
X the Xpenditure, grown quite gigantic.
Y are the Young men, whom nobody thought about—
Z is the Zeal that this victory brought about.

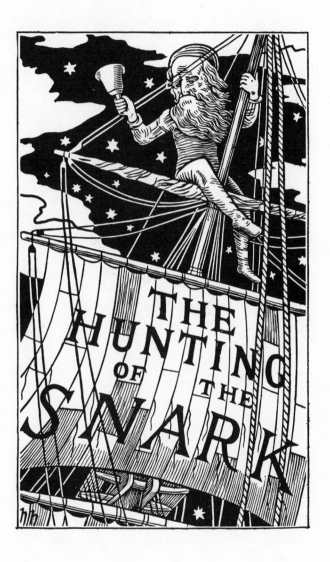

PREFACE

IF—and the thing is wildly possible—the charge of writing nonsense were ever brought against the author of this brief but instructive poem, it would be based, I feel convinced, on the line,

" Then the bowsprit got mixed with the rudder sometimes."

In view of this painful possibility, I will not (as I might) appeal indignantly to my other writings as a proof that I am incapable of such a deed : I will not (as I might) point to the strong moral purpose of this poem itself, to the arithmetical principles so cautiously inculcated in it, or to its noble teachings in Natural History—I will take the more prosaic course of simply explaining how it happened.

The Bellman, who was almost morbidly sensitive about appearances, used to have the bowsprit unshipped once or twice a week to be revarnished, and it more than once happened, when the time came for replacing it, that no one on board could remember which end of the ship it belonged to. They knew it was not of the slightest use to appeal to the Bellman about it—he would only refer to his Naval Code, and read out in pathetic tones Admiralty Instructions which none of them had ever been able to understand—so it

Preface

generally ended in its being fastened on anyhow, across the rudder. The helmsman [1] used to stand by with tears in his eyes : *he* knew it was all wrong, but alas ! Rule 42 of the Code, "*No one shall speak to the Man at the Helm*," had been completed by the Bellman himself with the words "*and the Man at the Helm shall speak to no one*." So remonstrance was impossible, and no steering could be done till the next varnishing day. During these bewildering intervals the ship usually sailed backwards.

As this poem is to some extent connected with the lay of the Jabberwock, let me take this opportunity of answering a question that has often been asked me, how to pronounce "slithy toves." The "i" in "slithy" is long, as in "writhe"; and "toves" is pronounced so as to rhyme with "groves." Again, the first "o" in "borogoves" is pronounced like the "o" in "borrow." I have heard people try to give it the sound of the "o" in "worry." Such is Human Perversity.

This also seems a fitting occasion to notice the other hard words in that poem. Humpty-Dumpty's theory, of two meanings packed into one word like a portmanteau, seems to me the right explanation for all.

For instance, take the two words "fuming" and "furious." Make up your mind that you will say both words, but leave it unsettled which you will say first. Now open your mouth and speak. If your thoughts incline ever so little towards "fuming," you will say "fuming-furious"; if they turn, by even a hair's breadth, towards "furious," you will say "furious-

---

[1] This office was usually undertaken by the Boots, who found in it a refuge from the Baker's constant complaints about the insufficient blacking of his three pair of boots.

Preface

fuming "; but if you have that rarest of gifts, a perfectly balanced mind, you will say " frumious."

Supposing that, when Pistol uttered the well-known words—

"Under which king, Bezonian ?   Speak or die !"

Justice Shallow had felt certain that it was either William or Richard, but had not been able to settle which, so that he could not possibly say either name before the other, can it be doubted that, rather than die, he would have gasped out " Rilchiam ! "

Inscribed to a dear Child:
in memory of golden summer hours
and whispers of a summer sea

(ACROSTIC)

GIRT with a boyish garb for boyish task,
　　Eager she wields her spade : yet loves as well
Rest on a friendly knee, intent to ask
　　　　The tale he loves to tell.

Rude spirits of the seething outer strife,
　　Unmeet to read her pure and simple spright,
Deem, if you list, such hours a waste of life
　　　　Empty of all delight !

Chat on, sweet Maid, and rescue from annoy
　　Hearts that by wiser talk are unbeguiled.
Ah, happy he who owns that tenderest joy,
　　　　The heart-love of a child !

Away, fond thoughts, and vex my soul no more !
　　Work claims my wakeful nights, my busy days—
Albeit bright memories of that sunlit shore
　　　　Yet haunt my dreaming gaze !

THE HUNTING OF THE SNARK

An Agony, in Eight Fits

Fit the First

THE LANDING

" Just the place for a Snark ! " the Bellman cried,
    As he landed his crew with care;
Supporting each man on the top of the tide
    By a finger entwined in his hair.

" Just the place for a Snark !   I have said it twice :
    That alone should encourage the crew.
Just the place for a Snark !   I have said it thrice :
    What I tell you three times is true."

The crew was complete : it included a Boots—
    A maker of Bonnets and Hoods—
A Barrister, brought to arrange their disputes—
    And a Broker, to value their goods.

A Billiard-marker, whose skill was immense,
    Might perhaps have won more than his share—
But a Banker, engaged at enormous expense,
    Had the whole of their cash in his care.

271

SUPPORTING EACH MAN ON THE TOP OF THE TIDE

The Landing

There was also a Beaver, that paced on the deck,
    Or would sit making lace in the bow :
And had often (the Bellman said) saved them from
      wreck,
    Though none of the sailors knew how.

There was one who was famed for the number of things
    He forgot when he entered the ship :
His umbrella, his watch, all his jewels and rings,
    And the clothes he had bought for the trip.

He had forty-two boxes, all carefully packed,
    With his name painted clearly on each :
But, since he omitted to mention the fact,
    They were all left behind on the beach.

The loss of his clothes hardly mattered, because
    He had seven coats on when he came,
With three pair of boots——but the worst of it was,
    He had wholly forgotten his name.

He would answer to " Hi ! " or to any loud cry,
    Such as " Fry me ! " or " Fritter my wig ! "
To " What-you-may-call-um ! " or " What-was-his-
      name ! "
    But especially " Thing-um-a-jig ! "

While, for those who preferred a more forcible word,
    He had different names from these :
His intimate friends called him " Candle-ends,"
    And his enemies " Toasted-cheese."

" His form is ungainly——his intellect small——"
    (So the Bellman would often remark)

HE HAD WHOLLY FORGOTTEN HIS NAME

The Landing

" But his courage is perfect !   And that, after all,
   Is the thing that one needs with a Snark."

He would joke with hyænas, returning their stare
   With an impudent wag of the head :
And he once went a walk, paw-in-paw, with a bear,
   " Just to keep up its spirits," he said.

He came as a Baker : but owned when too late—
   And it drove the poor Bellman half-mad—
He could only bake Bridecake——for which, I may
      state,
   No materials were to be had.

The last of the crew needs especial remark,
   Though he looked an incredible dunce :
He had just one idea——but, that one being " Snark,"
   The good Bellman engaged him at once.

He came as a Butcher : but gravely declared,
   When the ship had been sailing a week,
He could only kill Beavers. The Bellman looked
      scared,
   And was almost too frightened to speak :

But at length he explained, in a tremulous tone,
   There was only one Beaver on board ;
And that was a tame one he had of his own,
   Whose death would be deeply deplored.

The Beaver, who happened to hear the remark,
   Protested, with tears in its eyes,
That not even the rapture of hunting the Snark
   Could atone for that dismal surprise !

THE BEAVER KEPT LOOKING THE OPPOSITE WAY

The Landing

It strongly advised that the Butcher should be
  Conveyed in a separate ship :
But the Bellman declared that would never agree
  With the plans he had made for the trip :

Navigation was always a difficult art,
  Though with only one ship and one bell :
And he feared he must really decline, for his part,
  Undertaking another as well.

The Beaver's best course was, no doubt, to procure
  A second-hand dagger-proof coat——
So the Baker advised it——and next, to insure
  Its life in some Office of note :

This the Banker suggested, and offered for hire
  (On moderate terms), or for sale,
Two excellent Policies, one Against Fire,
  And one Against Damage From Hail.

Yet still, ever after that sorrowful day,
  Whenever the Butcher was by,
The Beaver kept looking the opposite way,
  And appeared unaccountably shy.

Fit the Second

THE BELLMAN'S SPEECH

The Bellman himself they all praised to the skies——
  Such a carriage, such ease and such grace !
Such solemnity, too ! One could see he was wise,
  The moment one looked in his face !

He had bought a large map representing the sea,
  Without the least vestige of land :
And the crew were much pleased when they found it
    to be
  A map they could all understand.

" What's the good of Mercator's North Poles and
    Equators,
  Tropics, Zones, and Meridian Lines ? "
So the Bellman would cry : and the crew would reply,
  " They are merely conventional signs !

" Other maps are such shapes, with their islands and
    capes !
  But we've got our brave Captain to thank "
(So the crew would protest) " that he's bought us the
    best——
  A perfect and absolute blank ! "

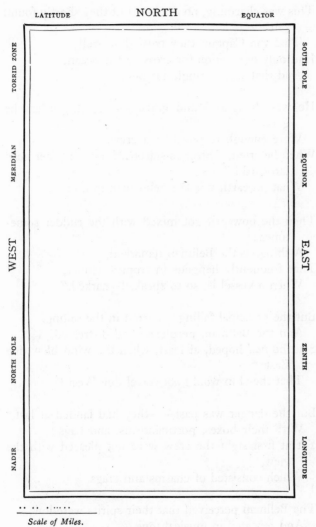

LATITUDE NORTH EQUATOR

TORRID ZONE

MERIDIAN

WEST

NORTH POLE

NADIR

SOUTH POLE

EQUINOX

EAST

ZENITH

LONGITUDE

Scale of Miles.

OCEAN-CHART.

The Hunting of the Snark

This was charming, no doubt : but they shortly found
      out
   That the Captain they trusted so well
Had only one notion for crossing the ocean,
   And that was to tingle his bell.

He was thoughtful and grave——but the orders he
      gave
   Were enough to bewilder a crew.
When he cried, " Steer to starboard, but keep her head
      larboard ! "
   What on earth was the helmsman to do ?

Then the bowsprit got mixed with the rudder some-
      times :
   A thing, as the Bellman remarked,
That frequently happens in tropical climes,
   When a vessel is, so to speak, " snarked."

But the principal failing occurred in the sailing,
   And the Bellman, perplexed and distressed,
Said he *had* hoped, at least, when the wind blew due
      East
   That the ship would *not* travel due West !

But the danger was past——they had landed at last,
   With their boxes, portmanteaus, and bags :
Yet at first sight the crew were not pleased with the
      view,
   Which consisted of chasms and crags.

The Bellman perceived that their spirits were low,
   And repeated in musical tone

The Bellman's Speech

Some jokes he had kept for a season of woe——
    But the crew would do nothing but groan.

He served out some grog with a liberal hand,
    And bade them sit down on the beach :
And they could not but own that their Captain looked
    grand,
    As he stood and delivered his speech.

" Friends, Romans, and countrymen, lend me your
    ears ! "
    (They were all of them fond of quotations :
So they drank to his health, and they gave him three
    cheers,
    While he served out additional rations.)

" We have sailed many months, we have sailed many
    weeks
    (Four weeks to the month you may mark),
But never as yet ('tis your Captain who speaks)
    Have we caught the least glimpse of a Snark !

" We have sailed many weeks, we have sailed many
    days
    (Seven days to the week I allow),
But a Snark, on the which we might lovingly gaze,
    We have never beheld till now !

" Come, listen, my men, while I tell you again
    The five unmistakable marks
By which you may know, wheresoever you go,
    The warranted genuine Snarks.

" Let us take them in order. The first is the taste,
    Which is meagre and hollow, but crisp :

The Hunting of the Snark

Like a coat that is rather too tight in the waist,
  With a flavour of Will-o'-the-wisp.

" Its habit of getting up late you'll agree
  That it carries too far, when I say
That it frequently breakfasts at five-o'clock tea,
  And dines on the following day.

" The third is its slowness in taking a jest,
  Should you happen to venture on one,
It will sigh like a thing that is deeply distressed :
  And it always looks grave at a pun.

" The fourth is its fondness for bathing-machines,
  Which it constantly carries about,
And believes that they add to the beauty of scenes——
  A sentiment open to doubt.

" The fifth is ambition.   It next will be right
  To describe each particular batch :
Distinguishing those that have feathers, and bite,
  From those that have whiskers, and scratch.

" For, although common Snarks do no manner of
    harm,
  Yet, I feel it my duty to say,
Some are Boojums——" The Bellman broke off in
    alarm,
  For the Baker had fainted away.

Fit the Third

THE BAKER'S TALE

THEY roused him with muffins—they roused him with
    ice—
  They roused him with mustard and cress—
They roused him with jam and judicious advice—
  They set him conundrums to guess.

When at length he sat up and was able to speak,
  His sad story he offered to tell;
And the Bellman cried " Silence ! not even a shriek ! "
  And excitedly tingled his bell.

There was silence supreme ! Not a shriek, not a
    scream,
  Scarcely even a howl or a groan,
As the man they called " Ho ! " told his story of woe
  In an antediluvian tone.

" My father and mother were honest, though poor——"
  " Skip all that ! " cried the Bellman in haste.
" If it once becomes dark, there's no chance of a
    Snark——
  We have hardly a minute to waste ! "

283

"BUT OH, BEAMISH NEPHEW, BEWARE OF THE DAY"

The Baker's Tale

" I skip forty years," said the Baker, in tears,
  " And proceed without further remark
To the day when you took me aboard of your ship
  To help you in hunting the Snark.

" A dear uncle of mine (after whom I was named)
  Remarked, when I bade him farewell——"
" Oh, skip your dear uncle ! " the Bellman exclaimed,
  As he angrily tingled his bell.

" He remarked to me then," said that mildest of men,
  " ' If your Snark be a Snark, that is right :
Fetch it home by all means——you may serve it with
    greens,
  And it's handy for striking a light.

" ' You may seek it with thimbles—and seek it with
    care ;
  You may hunt it with forks and hope ;
You may threaten its life with a railway-share ;
  You may charm it with smiles and soap—' "

(" That's exactly the method," the Bellman bold
  In a hasty parenthesis cried,
" That's exactly the way I have always been told
  That the capture of Snarks should be tried ! ")

" ' But oh, beamish nephew, beware of the day,
  If your Snark be a Boojum ! For then
You will softly and suddenly vanish away,
  And never be met with again ! '

" It is this, it is this that oppresses my soul,
  When I think of my uncle's last words :

The Hunting of the Snark

And my heart is like nothing so much as a bowl
   Brimming over with quivering curds !

" It is this, it is this——" " We have had that
   before ! "
The Bellman indignantly said.
And the Baker replied, " Let me say it once more.
   It is this, it is this that I dread !

" I engage with the Snark——every night after
   dark——
In a dreamy delirious fight :
I serve it with greens in those shadowy scenes,
   And I use it for striking a light ;

" But if ever I meet with a Boojum, that day,
   In a moment (of this I am sure),
I shall softly and suddenly vanish away—
   And the notion I cannot endure ! "

Fit the Fourth

THE HUNTING

The Bellman looked uffish, and wrinkled his brow.
  " If only you'd spoken before !
It's excessively awkward to mention it now,
  With the Snark, so to speak, at the door !

" We should all of us grieve, as you well may believe,
  If you never were met with again——
But surely, my man, when the voyage began,
  You might have suggested it then ?

" It's excessively awkward to mention it now—
  As I think I've already remarked."
And the man they called " Hi ! " replied, with a sigh,
  " I informed you the day we embarked.

" You may charge me with murder—or want of sense—
  (We are all of us weak at times) :
But the slightest approach to a false pretence
  Was never among my crimes !
287

The Hunting of the Snark

"I said it in Hebrew—I said it in Dutch—
  I said it in German and Greek;
But I wholly forgot (and it vexes me much)
  That English is what you speak!"

" 'Tis a pitiful tale," said the Bellman, whose face
  Had grown longer at every word;
"But, now that you've stated the whole of your case,
  More debate would be simply absurd.

"The rest of my speech" (he explained to his men)
  "You shall hear when I've leisure to speak it.
But the Snark is at hand, let me tell you again!
  'Tis your glorious duty to seek it!

"To seek it with thimbles, to seek it with care;
  To pursue it with forks and hope;
To threaten its life with a railway-share;
  To charm it with smiles and soap!

"For the Snark's a peculiar creature, that won't
  Be caught in a commonplace way.
Do all that you know, and try all that you don't:
  Not a chance must be wasted to-day!

"For England expects——I forbear to proceed:
  'Tis a maxim tremendous, but trite:
And you'd best be unpacking the things that you need
  To rig yourselves out for the fight."

Then the Banker endorsed a blank cheque (which he
    crossed),
  And changed his loose silver for notes.

"TO PURSUE IT WITH FORKS AND HOPE"

The Hunting of the Snark

The Baker with care combed his whiskers and hair,
  And shook the dust out of his coats.

The Boots and the Broker were sharpening a spade—
  Each working the grindstone in turn ;
But the Beaver went on making lace, and displayed
  No interest in the concern :

Though the Barrister tried to appeal to its pride,
  And vainly proceeded to cite
A number of cases, in which making laces
  Had been proved an infringement of right.

The maker of Bonnets ferociously planned
  A novel arrangement of bows :
While the Billiard-marker with quivering hand
  Was chalking the tip of his nose.

But the Butcher turned nervous, and dressed himself
    fine,
  With yellow kid gloves and a ruff——
Said he felt it exactly like going to dine,
  Which the Bellman declared was all " stuff."

" Introduce me, now there's a good fellow," he said,
  " If we happen to meet it together ! "
And the Bellman, sagaciously nodding his head,
  Said, " That must depend on the weather."

The Beaver went simply galumphing about,
  At seeing the Butcher so shy :
And even the Baker, though stupid and stout,
  Made an effort to wink with one eye.

The Hunting

" Be a man ! " said the Bellman in wrath, as he heard
The Butcher beginning to sob.
" Should we meet with a Jubjub, that desperate bird,
We shall need all our strength for the job ! "

Fit the Fifth

THE BEAVER'S LESSON

THEY sought it with thimbles, they sought it with care;
    They pursued it with forks and hope;
They threatened its life with a railway-share;
    They charmed it with smiles and soap.

Then the Butcher contrived an ingenious plan
    For making a separate sally;
And had fixed on a spot unfrequented by man,
    A dismal and desolate valley.

But the very same plan to the Beaver occurred:
    It had chosen the very same place;
Yet neither betrayed, by a sign or a word,
    The disgust that appeared in his face.

Each thought he was thinking of nothing but " Snark "
    And the glorious work of the day;
And each tried to pretend that he did not remark
    That the other was going that way.

But the valley grew narrow and narrower still,
    And the evening got darker and colder,
Till (merely from nervousness, not from goodwill)
    They marched along shoulder to shoulder.

The Beaver's Lesson

Then a scream, shrill and high, rent the shuddering
    sky,
    And they knew that some danger was near :
The Beaver turned pale to the tip of its tail,
    And even the Butcher felt queer.

He thought of his childhood, left far far behind—
    That blissful and innocent state—
The sound so exactly recalled to his mind
    A pencil that squeaks on a slate !

" 'Tis the voice of the Jubjub ! " he suddenly cried.
    (This man, that they used to call " Dunce.")
" As the Bellman would tell you," he added with pride,
    " I have uttered that sentiment once.

" 'Tis the note of the Jubjub ! Keep count, I entreat ;
    You will find I have told it you twice.
'Tis the song of the Jubjub ! The proof is complete,
    If only I've stated it thrice."

The Beaver had counted with scrupulous care,
    Attending to every word :
But it fairly lost heart, and outgrabe in despair,
    When the third repetition occurred.

It felt that, in spite of all possible pains,
    It had somehow contrived to lose count,
And the only thing now was to rack its poor brains
    By reckoning up the amount.

"'Two added to one—if that could but be done,"
    It said, " with one's fingers and thumbs ! "
Recollecting with tears how, in earlier years,
    It had taken no pains with its sums.

The Hunting of the Snark

" The thing can be done," said the Butcher, " I think.
   The thing must be done, I am sure.
The thing shall be done ! Bring me paper and ink,
   The best there is time to procure."

The Beaver brought paper, portfolio, pens,
   And ink in unfailing supplies :
While strange creepy creatures came out of their dens,
   And watched them with wondering eyes.

So engrossed was the Butcher, he heeded them not,
   As he wrote with a pen in each hand,
And explained all the while in a popular style
   Which the Beaver could well understand.

" Taking Three as the subject to reason about——
   A convenient number to state——
We add Seven, and Ten, and then multiply out
   By One Thousand diminished by Eight.

" The result we proceed to divide, as you see,
   By Nine Hundred and Ninety and Two :
Then subtract Seventeen, and the answer must be
   Exactly and perfectly true.

" The method employed I would gladly explain,
   While I have it so clear in my head,
If I had but the time and you had but the brain——
   But much yet remains to be said.

" In one moment I've seen what has hitherto been
   Enveloped in absolute mystery,
And without extra charge I will give you at large
   A Lesson in Natural History."

THE BEAVER BROUGHT PAPER, PORTFOLIO, PENS

The Hunting of the Snark

In his genial way he proceeded to say
  (Forgetting all laws of propriety,
And that giving instruction, without introduction,
  Would have caused quite a thrill in Society),

" As to temper the Jubjub's a desperate bird,
  Since it lives in perpetual passion :
Its taste in costume is entirely absurd——
  It is ages ahead of the fashion :

" But it knows any friend it has met once before :
  It never will look at a bribe :
And in charity-meetings it stands at the door,
  And collects——though it does not subscribe.

" Its flavour when cooked is more exquisite far
  Than mutton, or oysters, or eggs :
(Some think it keeps best in an ivory jar,
  And some, in mahogany kegs :)

" You boil it in sawdust : you salt it in glue :
  You condense it with locusts and tape :
Still keeping one principal object in view——
  To preserve its symmetrical shape."

The Butcher would gladly have talked till next day,
  But he felt that the Lesson must end,
And he wept with delight in attempting to say
  He considered the Beaver his friend.

While the Beaver confessed, with affectionate looks
  More eloquent even than tears,
It had learnt in ten minutes far more than all books
  Would have taught it in seventy years.

The Beaver's Lesson

They returned hand-in-hand, and the Bellman, unmanned
(For a moment) with noble emotion,
Said, " This amply repays all the wearisome days
We have spent on the billowy ocean ! "

Such friends, as the Beaver and Butcher became,
Have seldom if ever been known ;
In winter or summer, 'twas always the same——
You could never meet either alone.

And when quarrels arose——as one frequently finds
Quarrels will, spite of every endeavour——
The song of the Jubjub recurred to their minds,
And cemented their friendship for ever !

Fit the Sixth

THE BARRISTER'S DREAM

THEY sought it with thimbles, they sought it with care;
    They pursued it with forks and hope;
They threatened its life with a railway-share;
    They charmed it with smiles and soap.

But the Barrister, weary of proving in vain
    That the Beaver's lace-making was wrong,
Fell asleep, and in dreams saw the creature quite plain
    That his fancy had dwelt on so long.

He dreamed that he stood in a shadowy Court,
    Where the Snark, with a glass in its eye,
Dressed in gown, bands, and wig, was defending a pig
    On the charge of deserting its sty.

The Witnesses proved, without error or flaw,
    That the sty was deserted when found:
And the Judge kept explaining the state of the law
    In a soft under-current of sound.

The indictment had never been clearly expressed,
    And it seemed that the Snark had begun,
And had spoken three hours, before any one guessed
    What the pig was supposed to have done.

The Barrister's Dream

The Jury had each formed a different view
    (Long before the indictment was read),
And they all spoke at once, so that none of them knew
    One word that the others had said.

"You must know——" said the Judge: but the
    Snark exclaimed, " Fudge !
    That statute is obsolete quite !
Let me tell you, my friends, the whole question depends
    On an ancient manorial right.

" In the matter of Treason the pig would appear
    To have aided, but scarcely abetted :
While the charge of Insolvency fails, it is clear,
    If you grant the plea ' never indebted.'

" The fact of Desertion I will not dispute :
    But its guilt, as I trust, is removed
(So far as relates to the costs of this suit)
    By the Alibi which has been proved.

" My poor client's fate now depends on your votes."
    Here the speaker sat down in his place,
And directed the Judge to refer to his notes
    And briefly to sum up the case.

But the Judge said he never had summed up before ;
    So the Snark undertook it instead,
And summed it so well that it came to far more
    Than the Witnesses ever had said !

When the verdict was called for, the Jury declined,
    As the word was so puzzling to spell ;

"YOU MUST KNOW——" SAID THE JUDGE: BUT THE SNARK EXCLAIMED, "FUDGE!"

The Barrister's Dream

But they ventured to hope that the Snark wouldn't
    mind
    Undertaking that duty as we'l.

So the Snark found the verdict, although, as it owned,
    It was spent with the toils of the day :
When it said the word " GUILTY ! " the Jury all
    groaned,
    And some of them fainted away.

Then the Snark pronounced sentence, the Judge being
    quite
    Too nervous to utter a word :
When it rose to its feet, there was silence like night,
    And the fall of a pin might be heard.

" Transportation for life " was the sentence it gave,
    " And *then* to be fined forty pound."
The Jury all cheered, though the Judge said he feared
    That the phrase was not legally sound.

But their wild exultation was suddenly checked
    When the jailer informed them, with tears,
Such a sentence would have not the slightest effect,
    As the pig had been dead for some years.

The Judge left the Court, looking deeply disgusted :
    But the Snark, though a little aghast,
As the lawyer to whom the defence was intrusted,
    Went bellowing on to the last.

Thus the Barrister dreamed, while the bellowing seemed
    To grow every moment more clear :
Till he woke to the knell of a furious bell,
    Which the Bellman rang close at his ear.

SO GREAT WAS HIS FRIGHT THAT HIS WAISTCOAT TURNED WHITE

ffit tbe Seventb

THE BANKER'S FATE

THEY sought it with thimbles, they sought it with care;
  They pursued it with forks and hope;
They threatened its life with a railway-share;
  They charmed it with smiles and soap.

And the Banker, inspired with a courage so new
  It was matter for general remark,
Rushed madly ahead and was lost to their view
  In his zeal to discover the Snark.

But while he was seeking with thimbles and care,
  A Bandersnatch swiftly drew nigh
And grabbed at the Banker, who shrieked in despair,
  For he knew it was useless to fly.

He offered large discount—he offered a cheque
  (Drawn " to bearer ") for seven-pounds-ten:
But the Bandersnatch merely extended its neck
  And grabbed at the Banker again.

Without rest or pause—while those frumious jaws
  Went savagely snapping around—
He skipped and he hopped, and he floundered and
    flopped,
  Till fainting he fell to the ground.

The Hunting of the Snark

The Bandersnatch fled as the others appeared :
  Led on by that fear-stricken yell :
And the Bellman remarked, " It is just as I feared ! "
  And solemnly tolled on his bell.

He was black in the face, and they scarcely could trace
  The least likeness to what he had been :
While so great was his fright that his waistcoat turned
    white—
  A wonderful thing to be seen !

To the horror of all who were present that day,
  He uprose in full evening dress,
And with senseless grimaces endeavoured to say
  What his tongue could no longer express.

Down he sank in a chair—ran his hands through his
    hair—
  And chanted in mimsiest tones
Words whose utter inanity proved his insanity,
  While he rattled a couple of bones.

" Leave him here to his fate—it is getting so late ! "
  The Bellman exclaimed in a fright.
" We have lost half the day.   Any further delay,
  And we shan't catch a Snark before night ! "

ꓭit the Eighth

THE VANISHING

THEY sought it with thimbles, they sought it with care ;
  They pursued it with forks and hope ;
They threatened its life with a railway-share ;
  They charmed it with smiles and soap.

They shuddered to think that the chase might fail,
  And the Beaver, excited at last,
Went bounding along on the tip of its tail,
  For the daylight was nearly past.

" There is Thingumbob shouting ! " the Bellman said.
  " He is shouting like mad, only hark !
He is waving his hands, he is wagging his head,
  He has certainly found a Snark ! "

They gazed in delight, while the Butcher exclaimed,
  " He was always a desperate wag ! "
They beheld him—their Baker—their hero unnamed—
  On the top of a neighbouring crag,

Erect and sublime, for one moment of time.
  In the next, that wild figure they saw
(As if stung by a spasm) plunge into a chasm,
  While they waited and listened in awe.

THEN, SILENCE

The Vanishing

" It's a Snark ! " was the sound that first came to their
    ears,
  And seemed almost too good to be true.
Then followed a torrent of laughter and cheers :
  Then the ominous words, " It's a Boo—"

Then, silence. Some fancied they heard in the air
  A weary and wandering sigh
That sounded like " —jum ! " but the others declare
  It was only a breeze that went by.

They hunted till darkness came on, but they found
  Not a button, or feather, or mark,
By which they could tell that they stood on the ground
  Where the Baker had met with the Snark.

In the midst of the word he was trying to say,
  In the midst of his laughter and glee,
He had softly and suddenly vanished away——
  For the Snark *was* a Boojum, you see.

THE END

ACROSTICS, INSCRIPTIONS,
AND OTHER VERSES

ACROSTICS, INSCRIPTIONS, AND OTHER VERSES

ACROSTIC

(In a copy of Catherine Sinclair's *Holiday House* presented to the three Misses Liddell.)

LITTLE maidens, when you look
On this little story-book,
Reading with attentive eye
Its enticing history,
Never think that hours of play
Are your only HOLIDAY,
And that in a HOUSE of joy
Lessons serve but to annoy:
If in any HOUSE you find
Children of a gentle mind,
Each the others pleasing ever—
Each the others vexing never—
Daily work and pastime daily
In their order taking gaily—
Then be very sure that they
Have a life of HOLIDAY.

Christmas 1861.

TO THREE PUZZLED LITTLE GIRLS,
FROM THE AUTHOR

(In a copy of *Alice's Adventures* presented to the three Misses Drury.)

THREE little maidens weary of the rail,
Three pairs of little ears listening to a tale,
Three little hands held out in readiness,
For three little puzzles very hard to guess.
Three pairs of little eyes, open wonder-wide,
At three little scissors lying side by side.
Three little mouths that thanked an unknown Friend,
For one little book, he undertook to send.
Though whether they'll remember a friend, or book, or day—
In three little weeks is very hard to say.

August 1869.

DOUBLE ACROSTIC

(Sent to Miss E. M. Argles.)

I sing a place wherein agree
All things on land that fairest be,
All that is sweetest of the sea.

Nor can I break the silken knot
That binds my memory to the spot
And friends too dear to be forgot.

.　　.　　.　　.　　.

On rocky brow we loved to stand
And watch in silence, hand in hand,
The shadows veiling sea and land.　　　　B luf F

Then dropped the breeze ; no vessel passed :
So silent stood each taper mast,
You would have deemed it chained and fast. A ncho R

Above the blue and fleecy sky :
Below, the waves that quivering lie,
Like crisped curls of greenery.　　　　B roccol I

"A sail !" resounds from every lip.
Mizen, no, square-sail—ah, you trip !
Edith, it cannot be a ship !　　　　B arqu E

313

Double Acrostic

So home again from sea and beach,
One nameless feeling thrilling each.
A sense of beauty, passing speech.   A ppreciatio N

Let lens and tripod be unslung!
"Dolly!" 's the word on every tongue;
Dolly must sit, for she is young!   C   hil   D

Photography shall change her face,
Distort it with uncouth grimace—
Make her bloodthirsty, fierce, and base. O   diou   S

I end my song while scarce begun;
For I should want, ere all was done,
Four weeks to tell the tale of one: M   ont   H

And I should need as large a hand,
To paint a scene so wild and grand,
As he who traversed Egypt's land.   B   elzon   I

What say you, Edith?   Will it suit ye?
Reject it, if it fails in beauty:
You know your literary duty!   E   ditorshi   P

On the rail between Torquay and Guildford, Sep. 28,
    1869.

THREE LITTLE MAIDS

(In a copy of *Phantasmagoria* sent to the three Misses Drury
after they had been taken to the "German Reed Entertainment"
with the triple bill indicated in the last verse.)

THREE little maids, one winter day,
    While others went to feed,
To sing, to laugh, to dance, to play,
    More wisely went to—Reed.

Others, when lesson-time's begun,
    Go, half inclined to cry,
Some in a walk, some in a run;
    But *these* went in a—Fly.

I give to other little maids
    A smile, a kiss, a look,
Presents whose memory quickly fades;
    I give to these—a Book.

Happy Arcadia may blind,
    While *all abroad*, their eyes;
At home, this book (I trust) they'll find
    A *very catching* prize.

PUZZLE

(Sent to Mary, Ina, and Harriet or "Hartie" Watson. The letters omitted were to be discovered and inserted.)

WHEN . a . y and I . a told . a . . ie they'd seen a
  Small . . ea . u . e with . i . . . , dressed in crimson
    and blue,
. a . . ie cried " 'Twas a . ai . y ! Why, I . a and . a .y,
  I *should* have been happy if I had been you !"

Said . a . y "You wouldn't." Said I . a "You
    shouldn't—
  Since *you* can't be *us*, and *we* couldn't be *you*.
You are *one*, my dear . a . . ie, but *we* are a . a . . y,
  And a . i . . . e . i . tells us that *one* isn't *two*."

316

THREE CHILDREN

(Sent to Miss Mary Watson.)

THREE children (their names were so fearful
   You'll excuse me for leaving them out)
Sat silent, with faces all tearful—
      What *was* it about?

They were sewing, but needles are prickly,
   And fingers were cold as could be—
So they didn't get on very quickly,
      And they wept, silly Three!

"O Mother!" said they, "Guildford's not a
   Nice place for the winter, that's flat.
If you know any country that's hotter,
      Please take us to that!"

"Cease crying," said she, "little daughter!
   And when summer comes back with the flowers,
You shall roam by the edge of the water,
      In sunshiny hours."

"And in summer," said sorrowful Mary,
   "We shall hear the shrill scream of the train
That will bring that dear writer of fairy-
      tales hither again."

317

Three Children

(Now the person she meant to allude to
  Was—well! it is best to forget.
It was some one she *always* was rude to,
    Whenever they met.)

"It's my duty," their Mother continued,
  "To fill with things useful and right
Your small minds: if I put nothing in, you'd
    Be ignorant quite.

"But enough now of lessons and thinking:
  Your meal is quite ready, I see—
So attend to your eating and drinking,
    You thirsty young Three!"

Apr. 10, 1871.

318

TWO THIEVES

(In a copy of *Through the Looking-Glass* presented to the three Misses Drury.)

Two thieves went out to steal one day
    Thinking that no one knew it:
Three little maids, I grieve to say,
    Encouraged them to do it.

'Tis sad that little children should
    Encourage men in stealing!
But these, I've always understood,
    Have got no proper feeling.

An aged friend, who chanced to pass
    Exactly at the minute,
Said "Children!   Take this Looking-glass,
    And see your badness in it."

Jan. 11, 1872.

TWO ACROSTICS

(In a copy of Charlotte M. Yonge's *Little Lucy's Wonderful Globe*, given to Miss Ruth Dymes.)

ROUND the wondrous globe I wander wild,
Up and down-hill—Age succeeds to youth—
Toiling all in vain to find a child
Half so loving, half so dear as Ruth.

(In another book, given to Miss Margaret Dymes.)

MAIDENS, if a maid you meet
Always free from pout and pet,
Ready smile and temper sweet,
Greet my little Margaret.
And if loved by all she be
Rightly, not a pampered pet,
Easily you then may see
'Tis my little Margaret.

DOUBLE ACROSTIC

(On the names of the two Misses Bremer.)

Two little girls near London dwell,
More naughty than I like to tell.

1

Upon the lawn the hoops are seen:
The balls are rolling on the green.　　　　T ur F

2

The Thames is running deep and wide:
And boats are rowing on the tide.　　　　R ive R

3

In winter-time, all in a row,
The happy skaters come and go.　　　　I c E

4

"Papa!" they cry, "Do let us stay!"
He does not speak, but says they may.　　　N o D

5

"There is a land," he says, "my dear,
Which is too hot to skate, I fear."　　　A fric A

ACROSTIC

"ARE you deaf, Father William?" the young man said,
"Did you hear what I told you just now?
"Excuse me for shouting! Don't waggle your head
"Like a blundering, sleepy old cow!
"A little maid dwelling in Wallington Town,
"Is my friend, so I beg to remark:
"Do you think she'd be pleased if a book were sent down
"Entitled 'The Hunt of the Snark?'"

"Pack it up in brown paper!" the old man cried,
"And seal it with olive-and-dove.
"I command you to do it!" he added with pride,
"Nor forget, my good fellow, to send her beside
"Easter Greetings, and give her my love."

1876.

ACROSTIC

(In a copy of *Rhyme? and Reason?* given to the Misses Drury.)

"MAIDENS! if you love the tale,
   If you love the Snark,
Need I urge you, spread the sail,
Now, while freshly blows the gale,
   In your ocean-barque!

"English Maidens love renown,
   Enterprise, and fuss!"
Laughingly those Maidens frown;
Laughingly, with eyes cast down;
   And they answer thus:

"English Maidens fear to roam.
   Much we dread the dark;
Much we dread what ills might come,
If we left our English home,
   Even for a Snark!"

Apr. 6, 1876.

ACROSTIC

Love-lighted eyes, that will not start
At frown of rage or malice!
Uplifted brow, undaunted heart
Ready to dine on raspberry-tart
Along with fairy Alice!

In scenes as wonderful as if
She'd flitted in a magic skiff
Across the sea to Calais:
Be sure this night, in Fancy's feast,
Even till Morning gilds the east,
Laura will dream of Alice!

Perchance, as long years onward haste,
Laura will weary of the taste
Of Life's embittered chalice:
May she, in such a woeful hour,
Endued with Memory's mystic power,
Recall the dreams of Alice!

June 17, 1876.

TO M. A. B.

(In a copy of *Alice's Adventures* presented to Miss Marion Terry,
"Mary Ann Bessie Terry.")

THE royal MAB, dethroned, discrowned
　　By fairy rebels wild,
Has found a home on English ground,
　　And lives an English child.
I know it, Maiden, when I see
A fairy-tale upon your knee—
And note the page that idly lingers
Beneath those still and listless fingers—
And mark those dreamy looks that stray
To some bright vision far away,
Still seeking, in the pictured story,
The memory of a vanished glory.

ACROSTIC

(In a copy of *The Hunting of the Snark* presented to Miss **Marion** Terry.)

MAIDEN, though thy heart may quail
And thy quivering lip grow pale,
Read the Bellman's tragic tale!

Is it life of which it tells?
Of a pulse that sinks and swells
Never lacking chime of bells?

Bells of sorrow, bells of cheer,
Easter, Christmas, glad New Year,
Still they sound, afar, anear.

So may Life's sweet bells for thee,
In the summers yet to be,
Evermore make melody!

Aug. 15, 1876.

MADRIGAL

(Addressed to Miss May Forshall.)

HE shouts amain, he shouts again,
  (Her brother, fierce, as bluff King Hal),
"I tell you flat, I shall do that!"
  She softly whispers "'*May*' for '*shall*'!"

He wistful sighed one eventide
  (Her friend, that made this Madrigal),
"And shall I kiss you, pretty Miss!"
  Smiling she answered "'*May*' for '*shall*'!"

With eager eyes my reader cries,
  "Your friend must be indeed a val-
-uable child, so sweet, so mild!
  What do you call her?" "May For shall."

Dec. 24, 1877.

LOVE AMONG THE ROSES

ACROSTIC

"SEEK ye Love, ye fairy-sprites?
　Ask where reddest roses grow.
Rosy fancies he invites,
And in roses he delights,
　Have ye found him?"　"No!"

"Seek again, and find the boy
　In Childhood's heart, so pure and clear."
Now the fairies leap for joy,
　Crying, "Love is here!"

"Love has found his proper nest;
　And we guard him while he dozes
In a dream of peace and rest
　Rosier than roses."

Jan. 3, 1878.

TWO POEMS TO RACHEL DANIEL

(When invited by Dr. Daniel to contribute a poem on his infant daughter to the privately-printed *Garland of Rachel*, Lewis Carroll included the following lines in his reply, but afterwards sent the second poem.)

I

"Oh pudgy podgy pup!
Why *did* they wake you up?
Those crude nocturnal yells
Are *not* like silver bells:
Nor ever would recall
Sweet Music's 'dying fall.'
They rather bring to mind
The bitter winter wind
Through keyholes shrieking shrilly
When nights are dark and chilly:
Or like some dire duett,
Or quarrelsome quartette,
Of cats who chant their joys
With execrable noise,
And murder Time and Tune
To vex the patient Moon!"

Nov. 1880.

329

II

FOR *THE GARLAND OF RACHEL* (1881)

WHAT hand may wreathe thy natal crown,
    O tiny tender Spirit-blossom,
That out of Heaven hast fluttered down
    Into this Earth's cold bosom?

And how shall mortal bard aspire—
    All sin-begrimed and sorrow-laden—
To welcome, with the Seraph-choir,
    A pure and perfect Maiden?

Are not God's minstrels ever near,
    Flooding with joy the woodland mazes?
Which shall we summon, Baby dear,
    To carol forth thy praises?

With sweet sad song the Nightingale
    May soothe the broken hearts that languish
Where graves are green—the orphans' wail,
    The widow's lonely anguish:

The Turtle-dove with amorous coo
    May chide the blushing maid that lingers
To twine her bridal wreath anew
    With weak and trembling fingers:

330

For the Garland of Rachel

But human loves and human woes
    Would dim the radiance of thy glory—
Only the Lark such music knows
    As fits thy stainless story.

The world may listen as it will—
    She recks not, to the skies up-springing:
Beyond our ken she singeth still
    For very joy of singing.

THE LYCEUM

("I will add the verses I sent Agnes to commemorate our visit
to the Lyceum. I told her they had been found on a torn piece of
paper, of which I sent a facsimile." — From a letter to Miss Helen
Feilden.)

"İt is the lawyer's daughter,
    And she is grown so dear, so dear,
She costs me, in one evening,
    The income of a year!
'You can't have children's love,' she cried,
    'Unless you choose to fee 'em!'
'And what's your fee, child?' I replied.
    She simply said ——

"We saw 'The Cup.'"   I *hoped* she'd say,
    "I'm grateful to you, very."
She murmured, as she turned away,
    "That lovely [Ellen Terry.]
"Compared with her, the rest," she cried,
    "Are just like two or three um-
"berellas standing side by side!
    "Oh, gem of ——

"We saw Two Brothers.   I confess
    To *me* they seemed one man.
"Now which is which, child?   Can you guess?"
    She cried, "A-course I can!"
Bad puns like this I *always* dread,
    And am resolved to flee 'em.
And so I left her there, and fled;
    She *lives* at ——

1881.

332

ACROSTIC

Around my lonely hearth, to-night,
  Ghostlike the shadows wander:
Now here, now there, a childish sprite,
. Earthborn and yet as angel bright,
  Seems near me as I ponder.

Gaily she shouts: the laughing air
  Echoes her note of gladness—
Or bends herself with earnest care
Round fairy-fortress to prepare
Grim battlement or turret-stair—
  In childhood's merry madness!

New raptures still hath youth in store.
  Age may but fondly cherish
Half-faded memories of yore—
Up, craven heart! repine no more!
Love stretches hands from shore to shore:
  Love is, and shall not perish!

DREAMLAND

(The author's friend, C. E. Hutchinson, of Brasenose College, had a dream in which he saw a procession of the heroes of old moving past him to music which he was able to write down on waking. The verses were written by Lewis Carroll for this dream-music.)

WHEN midnight mists are creeping,
And all the land is sleeping,
Around me tread the mighty dead,
And slowly pass away.

Lo, warriors, saints, and sages,
From out the vanished ages,
With solemn pace and reverend face
Appear and pass away.

The blaze of noonday splendour,
The twilight soft and tender,
May charm the eye : yet they shall die,
Shall die and pass away.

But here, in Dreamland's centre,
No spoiler's hand may enter,
These visions fair, this radiance rare,
Shall never pass away.

I see the shadows falling,
The forms of old recalling;
Around me tread the mighty dead,
And slowly pass away.

1882.

TO MY PUPIL

DEDICATION TO *A TANGLED TALE*

(Acrostic, the name being given by the second letter in each line.)

BELOVED Pupil! Tamed by thee,
    Addish=, Subtrac=, Multiplica=tion,
Division, Fractions, Rule of Three,
    Attest thy deft manipulation!

Then onward! Let the voice of Fame
    From Age to Age repeat thy story,
Till thou hast won thyself a name
    Exceeding even Euclid's glory.

1885.

TO MY CHILD–FRIEND

DEDICATION TO *THE GAME OF LOGIC*

(Acrostic, the name being given by the second letter in each line.)

I CHARM in vain : for never again,
All keenly as my glance I bend,
    Will Memory, goddess coy,
    Embody for my joy
Departed days, nor let me gaze
    On thee, my Fairy Friend!

Yet could thy face, in mystic grace,
A moment smile on me, 'twould send
    Far-darting rays of light
    From Heaven athwart the night,
By which to read in very deed
    Thy spirit, sweetest Friend!

So may the stream of Life's long dream
Flow gently onward to its end,
    With many a floweret gay,
    A-down its willowy way :
May no sigh vex, no care perplex,
    My loving little Friend!

1886.

A RIDDLE

(Sent to Miss Gaynor Simpson.)

My first lends his aid when I plunge into trade :
　My second in jollifications :
My whole, laid on thinnish, imparts a neat finish
　To pictorial representations.

Answer.　Copal.

A LIMERICK

(Sent to Miss Vera Beringer, who was on holiday in the Isle of
Man.)

　　THERE was a young lady of station,
　　"I love man" was her sole exclamation ;
　　　　But when men cried, "You flatter,"
　　　　She replied, "Oh ! no matter,
　　Isle of Man is the true explanation."

RHYME? AND REASON?

(In a copy of the book presented to Miss Emmie Drury.)

"I'M EMInent in RHYME !" she said.
　"I make WRY Mouths of RYE-Meal gruel !"
The Poet smiled, and shook his head :
　"Is REASON, then, the missing jewel?"

A NURSERY DARLING

DEDICATION TO THE NURSERY 'ALICE,' 1889

(Acrostic, the name being given by the second letter in each line.)

A MOTHER'S breast :
Safe refuge from her childish fears,
From childish troubles, childish tears,
Mists that enshroud her dawning years!
See how in sleep she seems to sing
A voiceless psalm—an offering
Raised, to the glory of her King,
      In Love : for Love is Rest.

A Darling's kiss :
Dearest of all the signs that fleet
From lips that lovingly repeat
Again, again, their message sweet!
Full to the brim with girlish glee,
A child, a very child is she,
Whose dream of Heaven is still to be
      At Home : for Home is Bliss.

MAGGIE'S VISIT TO OXFORD

(June 9th to 13th, 1889)

(Written for Maggie Bowman, the child actress, who came to
Oxford with the *Bootles' Baby* company.)

WHEN Maggie once to Oxford came,
    On tour as "Bootles' Baby,"
She said, "I'll see this place of fame,
    However dull the day be."

So with her friend she visited
    The sights that it was rich in:
And first of all she popped her head
    Inside the Christ Church kitchen.

The Cooks around that little child
    Stood waiting in a ring:
And every time that Maggie smiled
    Those Cooks began to sing—
Shouting the Battle-cry of Freedom!

        "Roast, boil and bake,
        For Maggie's sake:
        Bring cutlets fine
        For *her* to dine,
        Meringues so sweet
        For her to eat—
        For Maggie may be
        Bootles' Baby!"

Maggie's Visit to Oxford

Then hand in hand in pleasant talk
    They wandered and admired
The Hall, Cathedral and Broad Walk,
    Till Maggie's feet were tired:

To Worcester Garden next they strolled,
    Admired its quiet lake:
Then to St. John, a college old,
    Their devious way they take.

In idle mood they sauntered round
    Its lawn so green and flat,
And in that garden Maggie found
    A lovely Pussy-Cat!

A quarter of an hour they spent
    In wandering to and fro:
And everywhere that Maggie went,
    The Cat was sure to go—
Shouting the Battle-cry of Freedom!

      "Maiow! Maiow!
      Come, make your bow,
      Take off your hats,
      Ye Pussy-Cats!
      And purr and purr,
      To welcome *her*,
      For Maggie may be
      Bootles' Baby!"

So back to Christ Church, not too late
    For them to go and see
A Christ Church undergraduate,
    Who gave them cakes and tea.

Maggie's Visit to Oxford

Next day she entered with her guide
   The garden called "Botanic,"
And there a fierce Wild Boar she spied,
   Enough to cause a panic:

But Maggie didn't mind, not she,
   She would have faced, alone,
That fierce wild boar, because, you see,
   The thing was made of stone.

On Magdalen walls they saw a face
   That filled her with delight,
A giant face, that made grimace
   And grinned with all its might.

A little friend, industrious,
   Pulled upwards all the while
The corner of its mouth, and thus
   He helped that face to smile!

"How nice," thought Maggie, "it would be
   If *I* could have a friend
To do that very thing for *me*
And make my mouth turn up with glee,
   By pulling at one end."

In Magdalen Park the deer are wild
   With joy, that Maggie brings
Some bread a friend had given the child,
   To feed the pretty things.

They flock round Maggie without fear:
   They breakfast and they lunch,

Maggie's Visit to Oxford

They dine, they sup, those happy deer—
  Still, as they munch and munch,
Shouting the Battle-cry of Freedom!

     "Yes, Deer are we,
     And dear is she!
     We love this child
     So sweet and mild:
     We all rejoice
     At Maggie's voice:
     We all are fed
     With Maggie's bread . . .
     For Maggie may be
     Bootles' Baby!"

They met a Bishop on their way . . .
  A Bishop large as life,
With loving smile that seemed to say
  "Will Maggie be my wife?"

Maggie thought *not*, because, you see,
  She was so *very* young,
And he was old as old could be . . .
  So Maggie held her tongue.

"My Lord, she's Bootles' Baby, we
  Are going up and down,"
Her friend explained, "that she may see
  The sights of Oxford Town."

"Now say what kind of place it is,"
  The Bishop gaily cried.
"The best place in the Provinces!"
  That little maid replied.

Maggie's Visit to Oxford

Away, next morning, Maggie went
  From Oxford town : but yet
The happy hours she there had spent
  She could not soon forget.

The train is gone, it rumbles on :
  The engine-whistle screams;
But Maggie deep in rosy sleep . . .
  And softly in her dreams,
Whispers the Battle-cry of Freedom.

      "Oxford, good-bye !"
      She seems to sigh.
      "You dear old City,
      With gardens pretty,
      And lanes and flowers,
      And college-towers,
      And Tom's great Bell . . .
      Farewell—farewell :
      For Maggie may be
      Bootles' Baby !"

MAGGIE B——

(Sent to Maggie Bowman with a copy of *Wanted—A King*, by Maggie Browne.)

WRITTEN by Maggie B——
Bought by me:
A present to Maggie B——
Sent by me:
But *who* can Maggie be?
Answered by me:
"She is she."

Aug. 13, 1891.

344

FROM
SYLVIE AND BRUNO

FROM

SYLVIE AND BRUNO

ACROSTIC

Is all our Life, then, but a dream
Seen faintly in the golden gleam
Athwart Time's dark resistless stream ?

Bowed to the earth with bitter woe,
Or laughing at some raree-show,
We flutter idly to and fro.

Man's little Day in haste we spend,
And, from its merry noontide, send
No glance to meet the silent end.

THE MAD GARDENER'S SONG

He thought he saw an Elephant,
　That practised on a fife :
He looked again, and found it was
　A letter from his wife.
" At length I realise," he said,
　" The bitterness of Life ! "

348

The Mad Gardener's Song

He thought he saw a Buffalo
  Upon the chimney-piece :
He looked again, and found it was
  His Sister's Husband's Niece.
" Unless you leave this house," he said,
  " I'll send for the Police ! "

He thought he saw a Rattlesnake
  That questioned him in Greek :
He looked again, and found it was
  The Middle of Next Week.
" The one thing I regret," he said,
  " Is that it cannot speak ! "

349

The Mad Gardener's Song

He thought he saw a Banker's Clerk
Descending from the bus:

He looked again, and found it was
   A Hippopotamus:
"If this should stay to dine," he said,
   "There won't be much for us!"

The Mad Gardener's Song

He thought he saw a Kangaroo
  That worked a coffee-mill:

He looked again, and found it was
  A Vegetable-Pill.
" Were I to swallow this," he said,
  " I should be very ill ! "
351

The Mad Gardener's Song

He thought he saw a Coach-and-Four

That stood beside his bed:

He looked again, and found it was

A Bear without a Head.

"Poor thing," he said, "poor silly thing!

It's waiting to be fed!"

352

The Mad Gardener's Song

He thought he saw an Albatross
    That fluttered round the lamp:

He looked again, and found it was
    A Penny-Postage-Stamp.
"You'd best be getting home," he said:
    "The nights are very damp!"

He thought he saw a Garden-Door
    That opened with a key:
He looked again, and found it was
    A Double Rule of Three:

353

The Mad Gardener's Song

"And all its mystery," he said,
    "Is clear as day to me!"

He thought he saw an Argument
    That proved he was the Pope:
He looked again, and found it was
    A Bar of Mottled Soap.
"A fact so dread," he faintly said,
    "Extinguishes all hope!"

354

THE WARDEN'S CHARM

LET craft, ambition, spite,
Be quenched in Reason's night,
Till weakness turn to might,
Till what is dark be light,
Till what is wrong be right!

PETER AND PAUL

"PETER is poor," said noble Paul,
  "And I have always been his friend:
And, though my means to *give* are small,
  At least I can afford to *lend*.
How few, in this cold age of greed,
  Do good, except on selfish grounds!
But I can feel for Peter's need,
  And I WILL LEND HIM FIFTY POUNDS!"

Peter and Paul

How great was Peter's joy to find
  His friend in such a genial vein !
How cheerfully the bond he signed,
  To pay the money back again !
" We can't," said Paul, " be too precise :
  'Tis best to fix the very day :
So, by a learned friend's advice,
  I've made it Noon, the Fourth of May."

" But this is April ! " Peter said.
  " The First of April, as I think.
Five little weeks will soon be fled :
  One scarcely will have time to wink !
Give me a year to speculate—
  To buy and sell—to drive a trade—"
Said Paul, " I cannot change the date.
  On May the Fourth it must be paid."

" Well, well ! " said Peter, with a sigh.
  " Hand me the cash, and I will go.
I'll form a Joint-Stock Company,
  And turn an honest pound or so."
" I'm grieved," said Paul, " to seem unkind :
  The money shall of course be lent :
But, for a week or two, I find
  It will not be convenient."

So, week by week, poor Peter came
  And turned in heaviness away ;
For still the answer was the same,
  " I cannot manage it to-day."
And now the April showers were dry—
  The five short weeks were nearly spent—

357

Peter and Paul

Yet still he got the old reply,
　"It is not quite convenient!"

The Fourth arrived, and punctual Paul
　Came, with his legal friend, at noon.
"I thought it best," said he, "to call:
　One cannot settle things too soon."
Poor Peter shuddered in despair:
　His flowing locks he wildly tore:

Peter and Paul

And very soon his yellow hair
  Was lying all about the floor.

The legal friend was standing by,
  With sudden pity half unmanned :
The tear-drop trembled in his eye,
  The signed agreement in his hand :
But when at length the legal soul
  Resumed its customary force,
" The Law," he said, " we can't control :
  Pay, or the Law must take its course ! "

Said Paul, " How bitterly I rue
  That fatal morning when I called !
Consider, Peter, what you do !
  You won't be richer when you're bald !
Think you, by rending curls away,
  To make your difficulties less ?
Forbear this violence, I pray :
  You do but add to my distress ! "

" Not willingly would I inflict,"
  Said Peter, " on that noble heart
One needless pang.   Yet why so strict ?
  Is *this* to act a friendly part ?
However legal it may be
  To pay what never has been lent,
This style of business seems to me
  Extremely inconvenient !

" No Nobleness of soul have I,
  Like *some* that in this Age are found ! "
(Paul blushed in sheer humility,
  And cast his eyes upon the ground.)

Peter and Paul

"This debt will simply swallow all,
    And make my life a life of woe!"
"Nay, nay, my Peter!" answered Paul.
    "You must not rail on Fortune so!

"You have enough to eat and drink:
    You are respected in the world:
And at the barber's, as I think,
    You often get your whiskers curled.
Though Nobleness you can't attain—
    To any very great extent—
The path of Honesty is plain,
    However inconvenient!"

"'Tis true," said Peter, "I'm alive:
    I keep my station in the world:
Once in the week I just contrive
    To get my whiskers oiled and curled.
But my assets are very low:
    My little income's overspent:
To trench on capital, you know,
    Is always inconvenient!"

"But pay your debts!" cried honest Paul.
    "My gentle Peter, pay your debts!
What matter if it swallows all
    That you describe as your 'assets'?
Already you're an hour behind:
    Yet Generosity is best.
It pinches me—but never mind:
    I WILL NOT CHARGE YOU INTEREST!"

"How good! How great!" poor Peter cried.
    "Yet I must sell my Sunday wig—
The scarf-pin that has been my pride—
    My grand piano—and my pig!"

Peter and Paul

Full soon his property took wings :
　　And daily, as each treasure went,
He sighed to find the state of things
　　Grow less and less convenient.

Weeks grew to months, and months to years :
　　Peter was worn to skin and bone :
And once he even said, with tears,
　　" Remember, Paul, that promised Loan ! "
Said Paul, " I'll lend you, when I can,
　　All the spare money I have got—
Ah, Peter, you're a happy man !
　　Yours is an enviable lot !

" I'm getting stout, as you may see :
　　It is but seldom I am well :
I cannot feel my ancient glee
　　In listening to the dinner-bell :
But you, you gambol like a boy,
　　Your figure is so spare and light :
The dinner-bell's a note of joy
　　To such a healthy appetite ! "

Said Peter, " I am well aware
　　Mine is a state of happiness :
And yet how gladly could I spare
　　Some of the comforts I possess !
What *you* call healthy appetite
　　I feel as Hunger's savage tooth :
And, when no dinner is in sight,
　　The dinner-bell's a sound of ruth !

" No scare-crow would accept this coat :
　　Such boots as these you seldom see.

361

Ah, Paul, a single five-pound-note
    Would make another man of me ! "
Said Paul, " It fills me with surprise
    To hear you talk in such a tone :
I fear you scarcely realise
    The blessings that are all your own !

" You're safe from being overfed :
    You're sweetly picturesque in rags :
You never know the aching head
    That comes along with money-bags :

362

Peter and Paul

And you have time to cultivate
   That best of qualities, Content—
For which you'll find your present state
   Remarkably convenient ! "

Said Peter, " Though I cannot sound
   The depths of such a man as you,
Yet in your character I've found
   An inconsistency or two.
You seem to have long years to spare
   When there's a promise to fulfil :
And yet how punctual you were
   In calling with that little bill ! "

" One can't be too deliberate,"
   Said Paul, " in parting with one's pelf.
With bills, as you correctly state,
   I'm punctuality itself.
A man may surely claim his dues :
   But, when there's money to be *lent*,
A man must be allowed to choose
   Such times as are convenient ! "

It chanced one day, as Peter sat
   Gnawing a crust—his usual meal—
Paul bustled in to have a chat,
   And grasped his hand with friendly zeal.
" I knew," said he, " your frugal ways :
   So, that I might not wound your pride
By bringing strangers in to gaze,
   I've left my legal friend outside !

" You well remember, I am sure,
   When first your wealth began to go,

And people sneered at one so poor,
  I never used my Peter so !
And when you'd lost your little all,
  And found yourself a thing despised,
I need not ask you to recall
  How tenderly I sympathised !

" Then the advice I've poured on you,
  So full of wisdom and of wit :
All given gratis, though 'tis true
  I might have fairly charged for it !

Peter and Paul

But I refrain from mentioning
  Full many a deed I might relate—
For boasting is a kind of thing
  That I particularly hate.

" How vast the total sum appears
  Of all the kindnesses I've done,
From Childhood's half-forgotten years
  Down to that Loan of April One !
That Fifty Pounds ! You little guessed
  How deep it drained my slender store :
But there's a heart within this breast,
  And I WILL LEND YOU FIFTY MORE ! "

" Not so," was Peter's mild reply,
  His cheeks all wet with grateful tears :
" No man recalls, so well as I,
  Your services in bygone years :
And this new offer, I admit,
  Is very very kindly meant—
Still, to avail myself of it
  Would not be quite convenient ! "

BRUNO'S SONG

Rise, oh, rise ! The daylight dies :
  The owls are hooting, ting, ting, ting !
Wake, oh, wake ! Beside the lake
  The elves are fluting, ting, ting, ting !
Welcoming our Fairy King,
  We sing, sing, sing.

Hear, oh, hear ! From far and near
  The music stealing, ting, ting, ting !
Fairy bells adown the dells
  Are merrily pealing, ting, ting, ting !
Welcoming our Fairy King,
  We ring, ring, ring.

See, oh, see ! On every tree
  What lamps are shining, ting, ting, ting !
They are eyes of fiery flies
  To light our dining, ting, ting, ting !

Bruno's Song

Welcoming our Fairy King,
  They swing, swing, swing.

Haste, oh, haste, to take and taste
  The dainties waiting, ting, ting, ting !
Honey-dew is stored——

THE THREE BADGERS

THERE be three Badgers on a mossy stone
 Beside a dark and covered way :
Each dreams himself a monarch on his throne,
  And so they stay and stay—
Though their old Father languishes alone,
  They stay, and stay, and stay.

There be three Herrings loitering around,
 Longing to share that mossy seat :
Each Herring tries to sing what she has found
  That makes Life seem so sweet.
Thus, with a grating and uncertain sound,
  They bleat, and bleat, and bleat.

The Mother-Herring, on the salt sea-wave,
 Sought vainly for her absent ones :
The Father-Badger, writhing in a cave,
  Shrieked out " Return, my sons !

The Three Badgers

You shall have buns," he shrieked, "if you'll behave !
 Yea, buns, and buns, and buns ! "

"I fear," said she, "your sons have gone astray.
 My daughters left me while I slept."
"Yes 'm," the Badger said : "it's as you say.
 "They should be better kept."
Thus the poor parents talked the time away,
 And wept, and wept, and wept.

"Oh, dear beyond our dearest dreams,
Fairer than all that fairest seems !
To feast the rosy hours away,
To revel in a roundelay !
 How blest would be
 A life so free—
Ipwergis-Pudding to consume,
And drink the subtle Azzigoom !

EACH IN HIS MOUTH A LIVING HERRING BORE

The Three Badgers

" And if, in other days and hours,
Mid other fluffs and other flowers,
The choice were given me how to dine—
' Name what thou wilt : it shall be thine ! '
      Oh, then I see
      The life for me—
Ipwergis-Pudding to consume,
And drink the subtle Azzigoom ! "

The Badgers did not care to talk to Fish :
  They did not dote on Herrings' songs :
They never had experienced the dish
    To which that name belongs :
" And oh, to pinch their tails," (this was their wish,)
  " With tongs, yea, tongs, and tongs ! "

" And are not these the Fish," the Eldest sighed,
  " Whose Mother dwells beneath the foam ? "
" They *are* the Fish ! " the Second one replied.
    " And they have left their home ! "
" Oh, wicked Fish," the Youngest Badger cried,
  " To roam, yea, roam, and roam ! "

Gently the Badgers trotted to the shore—
  The sandy shore that fringed the bay :
Each in his mouth a living Herring bore—
    Those aged ones waxed gay :
Clear rang their voices through the ocean's roar,
  " Hooray, hooray, hooray ! "

LADY MURIEL'S SONG

He stept so lightly to the land,
　All in his manly pride :
He kissed her cheek, he pressed her hand,
　Yet still she glanced aside.
" Too gay he seems," she darkly dreams,
　" Too gallant and too gay
To think of me—poor simple me—
　When he is far away ! "

" I bring my Love this goodly pearl
　Across the seas," he said :
" A gem to deck the dearest girl
　That ever sailor wed ! "
She clasps it tight : her eyes are bright :
　Her throbbing heart would say
" He thought of me—he thought of me—
　When he was far away ! "

The ship has sailed into the West :
　Her ocean-bird is flown :
A dull dead pain is in her breast,
　And she is weak and lone :
Yet there's a smile upon her face,
　A smile that seems to say

Lady Muriel's Song

" He'll think of me—he'll think of me—
    When he is far away !

" Though waters wide between us glide,
    Our lives are warm and near :
No distance parts two faithful hearts—
    Two hearts that love so dear :
And I will trust my sailor-lad,
    For ever and a day,
To think of me—to think of me—
    When he is far away ! "

FROM

SYLVIE AND BRUNO CONCLUDED

FROM

SYLVIE AND BRUNO CONCLUDED

ACROSTIC

(The name is given by the third letter in each line.)

DREAMS, that elude the Waker's frenzied grasp—
Hands, stark and still, on a dead Mother's breast,
Which nevermore shall render clasp for clasp,
Or deftly soothe a weeping Child to rest—
In suchlike forms me listeth to portray
My Tale, here ended. Thou delicious Fay—
The guardian of a Sprite that lives to tease thee—
Loving in earnest, chiding but in play
The merry mocking Bruno ! Who, that sees thee,
Can fail to love thee, Darling, even as I ?—
My sweetest Sylvie, we must say " Good-bye ! "

THE KING-FISHER SONG

KING FISHER courted Lady Bird——
Sing Beans, sing Bones, sing Butterflies!
  "Find me my match," he said,
  "With such a noble head——
With such a beard, as white as curd——
  With such expressive eyes!"

"Yet pins have heads," said Lady Bird——
Sing Prunes, sing Prawns, sing Primrose-Hill!

The King-Fisher Song

" And, where you stick them in,
     They stay, and thus a pin
Is very much to be preferred
     To one that's never still ! "

" Oysters have beards," said Lady Bird——
Sing Flies, sing Frogs, sing Fiddle-strings !
     " I love them, for I know
     They never chatter so :
They would not say one single word——
     Not if you crowned them Kings ! "

" Needles have eyes," said Lady Bird——
Sing Cats, sing Corks, sing Cowslip-tea !
     " And they are sharp—just what
     Your Majesty is *not :*
So get you gone—'tis too absurd
     To come a-courting *me* ! "

MATILDA JANE

"Matilda Jane, you never look
At any toy or picture-book :
I show you pretty things in vain—
You must be blind, Matilda Jane !

"I ask you riddles, tell you tales,
But *all* our conversation fails :
You *never* answer me again—
I fear you're dumb, Matilda Jane !

"Matilda, darling, when I call,
You never seem to hear at all :
I shout with all my might and main—
But you're *so* deaf, Matilda Jane !

Matilda Jane

" Matilda Jane, you needn't mind :
For, though you're deaf, and dumb, and blind,
There's *some one* loves you, it is plain—
And that is *me*, Matilda Jane ! "

WHAT TOTTLES MEANT

" ONE thousand pounds per annuum
Is not so bad a figure, come ! "
Cried Tottles. " And I tell you, flat,
A man may marry well on that !
To say ' the Husband needs the Wife '
Is *not* the way to represent it.
The crowning joy of Woman's life
Is *Man !* " said Tottles (and he meant it).

The blissful Honeymoon is past :
The Pair have settled down at last :
Mamma-in-law their home will share,
And make their happiness her care.
" Your income is an ample one :
Go it, my children ! " (And they went it).
" I *rayther* think this kind of fun
Won't last ! " said Tottles (and he meant it).

What Tottles Meant

They took a little country-box——
A box at Covent Garden also:
They lived a life of double-knocks,
Acquaintances began to call so:
Their London house was much the same
(It took three hundred, clear, to rent it):
"Life is a very jolly game!"
Cried happy Tottles (and he meant it).

"Contented with a frugal lot"
(He always used that phrase at Gunter's),
He bought a handy little yacht—
A dozen serviceable hunters—
The fishing of a Highland Loch—
A sailing-boat to circumvent it—
"The sounding of that Gaelic 'och'
Beats *me*!" said Tottles (and he meant it).

But oh, the worst of human ills
(Poor Tottles found) are "little bills"!
And, with no balance in the Bank,
What wonder that his spirits sank?
Still, as the money flowed away,
He wondered how on earth she spent it.
"You cost me twenty pounds a day,
At least!" cried Tottles (and he meant it).

She sighed. "Those Drawing Rooms, you know!
I really never thought about it:
Mamma declared we ought to go—
We should be Nobodies without it.
That diamond circlet for my brow—
I quite believed that *she* had sent it,
Until the Bill came in just now——"
"*Viper*!" cried Tottles (and he meant it).

What Tottles Meant

Poor Mrs. T. could bear no more,
But fainted flat upon the floor.
Mamma-in-law, with anguish wild,
Seeks, all in vain, to rouse her child.
" Quick ! Take this box of smelling-salts !
Don't scold her, James, or you'll repent it,
She's a *dear* girl, with all her faults——"
" She *is* ! " groaned Tottles (and he meant it).

" I was a donkey," Tottles cried,
" To choose your daughter for my bride !
'Twas *you* that bid us cut a dash !
'Tis *you* have brought us to this smash !
You don't suggest one single thing
That can in any way prevent it—
Then what's the use of arguing ?
Shut up ! " cried Tottles (and he meant it).

" And, now the mischief's done, perhaps
You'll kindly go and pack your traps ?
Since *two* (your daughter and your son)
Are Company, but *three* are none.
A course of saving we'll begin :
When change is needed, *I'll* invent it :
Don't think to put *your* finger in
This pie ! " cried Tottles (and he meant it).

See now this couple settled down
In quiet lodgings, out of town :
Submissively the tearful wife
Accepts a plain and humble life :
Yet begs one boon on bended knee :
" My ducky-darling, don't resent it !
Mamma might come for two or three——"
" NEVER ! " yelled Tottles. And he meant it.

384

THE LITTLE MAN THAT HAD A LITTLE GUN

IN stature the Manlet was dwarfish—
  No burly big Blunderbore he :
And he wearily gazed on the crawfish
  His Wifelet had dressed for his tea.
" Now reach me, sweet Atom, my gunlet,
  And hurl the old shoelet for luck :
Let me hie to the bank of the runlet,
          And shoot thee a Duck ! "

She has reached him his minikin gunlet :
  She has hurled the old shoelet for luck :
She is busily baking a bunlet,
  To welcome him home with his Duck.
On he speeds, never wasting a wordlet,
  Though thoughtlets cling, closely as wax,
To the spot where the beautiful birdlet
          So quietly quacks.

Where the Lobsterlet lurks, and the Crablet
    So slowly and sleepily crawls:
Where the Dolphin's at home, and the Dablet
    Pays long ceremonious calls:
Where the Grublet is sought by the Froglet:
    Where the Frog is pursued by the Duck:
Where the Ducklet is chased by the Doglet—
        So runs the world's luck!

He has loaded with bullet and powder:
    His footfall is noiseless as air:
But the Voices grow louder and louder,
    And bellow, and bluster, and blare.
They bristle before him and after,
    They flutter above and below,
Shrill shriekings of lubberly laughter,
        Weird wailings of woe!

They echo without him, within him:
    They thrill through his whiskers and beard:
Like a teetotum seeming to spin him,

With sneers never hitherto sneered.
" Avengement," they cry, " on our Foelet !
Let the Manikin weep for our wrongs !
Let us drench him, from toplet to toelet,
      With Nursery-Songs !

" He shall muse upon ' Hey ! Diddle ! Diddle !
  On the Cow that surmounted the Moon :
He shall rave of the Cat and the Fiddle,
  And the Dish that eloped with the Spoon :
And his soul shall be sad for the Spider,
  When Miss Muffet was sipping her whey,
That so tenderly sat down beside her,
      And scared her away !

" The music of Midsummer-madness
  Shall sting him with many a bite,
Till, in rapture of rollicking sadness,
  He shall groan with a gloomy delight :
He shall swathe him, like mists of the morning,
  In platitudes luscious and limp,

Such as deck, with a deathless adorning,
    The Song of the Shrimp !

" When the Ducklet's dark doom is decided,
  We will trundle him home in a trice :
And the banquet, so plainly provided,
  Shall round into rose-buds and rice :
In a blaze of pragmatic invention
  He shall wrestle with Fate, and shall reign :
But he has not a friend fit to mention,
    So hit him again ! "

He has shot it, the delicate darling !
  And the Voices have ceased from their strife :
Not a whisper of sneering or snarling,
  As he carries it home to his wife :
Then, cheerily champing the bunlet
  His spouse was so skilful to bake,
He hies him once more to the runlet,
    To fetch her the Drake !

A SONG OF LOVE

SAY, what is the spell, when her fledgelings are
cheeping,
   That lures the bird home to her nest?
Or wakes the tired mother, whose infant is weeping,
   To cuddle and croon it to rest?
What's the magic that charms the glad babe in her
arms,
   Till it coos with the voice of the dove?
'Tis a secret, and so let us whisper it low—
   And the name of the secret is Love!

         For I think it is Love,
         For I feel it is Love,
   For I'm sure it is nothing but Love!

Say, whence is the voice that, when anger is burning,
   Bids the whirl of the tempest to cease?
That stirs the vexed soul with an aching—a yearning
   For the brotherly hand-grip of peace?
Whence the music that fills all our being—that thrills
   Around us, beneath, and above?
'Tis a secret: none knows how it comes, how it goes:
   But the name of the secret is Love!

THE NAME OF THE SECRET IS LOVE!

A Song of Love

For I think it is Love,
For I feel it is Love,
For I'm sure it is nothing but Love !

Say, whose is the skill that paints valley and hill,
   Like a picture so fair to the sight ?
That flecks the green meadow with sunshine and
     shadow,
   Till the little lambs leap with delight ?
'Tis a secret untold to hearts cruel and cold,
   Though 'tis sung, by the angels above,
In notes that ring clear for the ears that can hear—
   And the name of the secret is Love !

For I think it is Love,
For I feel it is Love,
For I'm sure it is nothing but Love !

Little Birds are dining
    Warily and well
      Hid in mossy cell :
Hid, I say, by waiters
Gorgeous in their gaiters—
    I've a Tale to tell.

Little Birds are feeding
    Justices with jam,
      Rich in frizzled ham :
Rich, I say, in oysters
Haunting shady cloisters—
    That is what I am.

Little Birds are teaching
    Tigresses to smile,
      Innocent of guile :

The Pig-Tale

Smile, I say, not smirkle—
Mouth a semicircle,
      That's the proper style !

Little Birds are sleeping
      All among the pins,
      Where the loser wins :
Where, I say, he sneezes,
When and how he pleases—
      So the Tale begins.

THERE was a Pig that sat alone
    Beside a ruined Pump :
By day and night he made his moan—
It would have stirred a heart of stone
To see him wring his hoofs and groan,
    Because he could not jump.

A certain Camel heard him shout—
    A Camel with a hump.
" Oh, is it Grief, or is it Gout ?
What is this bellowing about ? "
That Pig replied, with quivering snout,
    " Because I cannot jump ! "

That Camel scanned him, dreamy-eyed.
    " Methinks you are too plump.
I never knew a Pig so wide—
That wobbled so from side to side—
Who could, however much he tried,
    Do such a thing as *jump !*

" Yet mark those trees, two miles away,
    All clustered in a clump :

If you could trot there twice a day,
Nor ever pause for rest or play,
In the far future—Who can say ?—
　　You may be fit to jump."

That Camel passed, and left him there
　　Beside the ruined Pump.
Oh, horrid was that Pig's despair !
His shrieks of anguish filled the air.
He wrung his hoofs, he rent his hair,
　　Because he could not jump.

There was a Frog that wandered by—
　　A sleek and shining lump :
Inspected him with fishy eye,
And said " O Pig, what makes you cry ? "

The Pig-Tale

And bitter was that Pig's reply,
  " Because I cannot jump ! "

That Frog he grinned a grin of glee,
  And hit his chest a thump.
" O Pig," he said, " be ruled by me,
And you shall see what you shall see.
This minute, for a trifling fee,
  I'll teach you how to jump !

" You may be faint from many a fall,
  And bruised by many a bump :
But, if you persevere through all,
And practise first on something small,
Concluding with a ten-foot wall,
  You'll find that you *can* jump ! "

That Pig looked up with joyful start :
  " Oh, Frog, you *are* a trump !
Your words have healed my inward smart—
Come, name your fee and do your part :
Bring comfort to a broken heart,
  By teaching me to jump ! "

" My fee shall be a mutton-chop,
  My goal this ruined Pump.
Observe with what an airy flop
I plant myself upon the top !
Now bend your knees and take a hop,
  For that's the way to jump ! "

Uprose that Pig, and rushed, full whack,
  Against the ruined Pump :
Rolled over like an empty sack,
And settled down upon his back,
While all his bones at once went " Crack ! "
  It was a fatal jump.

Little Birds are writing
   Interesting books,
    To be read by cooks :
Read, I say, not roasted—
Letterpress, when toasted,
   Loses its good looks.

Little Birds are playing
　　Bagpipes on the shore,
　　Where the tourists snore :
" Thanks ! " they cry.　" 'Tis
　　thrilling
Take, oh, take this shilling !
　　Let us have no more ! "

Little Birds are bathing
　　Crocodiles in cream,
　　Like a happy dream :
Like, but not so lasting—
Crocodiles, when fasting,
　　Are not all they seem !

That Camel passed, as day grew dim
   Around the ruined Pump.
" O broken heart !   O broken limb !
It needs," that Camel said to him,
" Something more fairy-like and slim,
   To execute a jump ! "

That Pig lay still as any stone,
   And could not stir a stump :
Nor ever, if the truth were known,
Was he again observed to moan,
Nor ever wring his hoofs and groan,
   Because he could not jump.

That Frog made no remark, for he
   Was dismal as a dump :

The Pig-Tale

He knew the consequence must be
That he would never get his fee—
And still he sits, in miserie,
    Upon that ruined Pump!

Little Birds are choking
    Baronets with bun,
    Taught to fire a gun :
Taught, I say, to splinter
Salmon in the winter—
    Merely for the fun.

Little Birds are hiding
    Crimes in carpet-bags,
    Blessed by happy stags :
Blessed, I say, though beaten—
Since our friends are eaten
    When the memory flags.

Little Birds are tasting
    Gratitude and gold,
    Pale with sudden cold :
Pale, I say, and wrinkled—
When the bells have tinkled,
    And the Tale is told.

THREE SUNSETS
AND OTHER POEMS

THREE SUNSETS
AND OTHER POEMS

THREE SUNSETS

HE saw her once, and in the glance,
   A moment's glance of meeting eyes,
His heart stood still in sudden trance :
   He trembled with a sweet surprise—
All in the waning light she stood,
The star of perfect womanhood.

That summer-eve his heart was light :
   With lighter step he trod the ground :
And life was fairer in his sight,
   And music was in every sound :
He blessed the world where there could be
So beautiful a thing as she.

There once again, as evening fell
   And stars were peering overhead,
Two lovers met to bid farewell :
   The western sun gleamed faint and red,
Lost in a drift of purple cloud
That wrapped him like a funeral-shroud.

Long time the memory of that night—
   The hand that clasped, the lips that kissed,
The form that faded from his sight
   Slow sinking through the tearful mist—

Three Sunsets

In dreamy music seemed to roll
Through the dark chambers of his soul.

So after many years he came
   A wanderer from a distant shore :
The street, the house, were still the same,
   But those he sought were there no more :
His burning words, his hopes and fears,
Unheeded fell on alien ears.

Only the children from their play
   Would pause the mournful tale to hear,
Shrinking in half-alarm away,
   Or, step by step, would venture near
To touch with timid curious hands
That strange wild man from other lands.

He sat beside the busy street,
   There, where he last had seen her face ;
And thronging memories, bitter-sweet,
   Seemed yet to haunt the ancient place :
Her footfall ever floated near :
Her voice was ever in his ear.

He sometimes, as the daylight waned
   And evening mists began to roll,
In half-soliloquy complained
   Of that black shadow on his soul,
And blindly fanned, with cruel care,
The ashes of a vain despair.

The summer fled : the lonely man
   Still lingered out the lessening days :
Still, as the night drew on, would scan
   Each passing face with closer gaze—

Three Sunsets

Till, sick at heart, he turned away,
And sighed " She will not come to-day."

So by degrees his spirit bent
    To mock its own despairing cry,
In stern self-torture to invent
    New luxuries of agony,
And people all the vacant space
With visions of her perfect face.

Then for a moment she was nigh,
    He heard no step, but she was there ;
As if an angel suddenly
    Were bodied from the viewless air,
And all her fine ethereal frame
Should fade as swiftly as it came.

So, half in fancy's sunny trance,
    And half in misery's aching void,
With set and stony countenance
    His bitter being he enjoyed,
And thrust for ever from his mind
The happiness he could not find.

As when the wretch, in lonely room,
    To selfish death is madly hurled,
The glamour of that fatal fume
    Shuts out the wholesome living world—·
So all his manhood's strength and pride
One sickly dream had swept aside.

Yea, brother, and we passed him there,
    But yesterday, in merry mood,
And marvelled at the lordly air
    That shamed his beggar's attitude,

Three Sunsets

Nor heeded that ourselves might be
Wretches as desperate as he ;

Who let the thought of bliss denied
   Make havoc of our life and powers,
And pine, in solitary pride,
   For peace that never shall be ours,
Because we will not work and wait
In trustful patience for our fate.

And so it chanced once more that she
   Came by the old familiar spot :
The face he would have died to see
   Bent o'er him, and he knew it not ;
Too rapt in selfish grief to hear,
Even when happiness was near.

And pity filled her gentle breast
   For him that would not stir nor speak,
The dying crimson of the west,
   That faintly tinged his haggard cheek,
Fell on her as she stood, and shed
A glory round the patient head.

Ah, let him wake !   The moments fly :
   This awful tryst may be the last.
And see, the tear, that dimmed her eye,
   Had fallen on him ere she passed—
She passed : the crimson paled to gray :
And hope departed with the day.

The heavy hours of night went by,
   And silence quickened into sound,

Three Sunsets

And light slid up the eastern sky,
   And life began its daily round—
But light and life for him were fled :
His name was numbered with the dead.

Nov. 1861.

THE PATH OF ROSES

[Written soon after the Crimean War, when the name of Florence Nightingale had already become a household-word.]

In the dark silence of an ancient room,
Whose one tall window fronted to the West,
Where, through laced tendrils of a hanging vine,
The sunset-glow was fading into night,
Sat a pale Lady, resting weary hands
Upon a great clasped volume, and her face
Within her hands. Not as in rest she bowed,
But large hot tears were coursing down her cheek,
And her low-panted sobs broke awefully
Upon the sleeping echoes of the night.
  Soon she unclasp'd the volume once again,
And read the words in tone of agony,
As in self-torture, weeping as she read :—

> " *He crowns the glory of his race :*
> *He prayeth but in some fit place*
> *To meet his foeman face to face :*

> " *And, battling for the True, the Right,*
> *From ruddy dawn to purple night,*
> *To perish in the midmost fight :*

The Path of Roses

" Where hearts are fierce and hands are strong,
Where peals the bugle loud and long,
Where blood is dropping in the throng :

" Still, with a dim and glazing eye,
To watch the tide of victory,
To hear in death the battle-cry :

" Then, gathered grandly to his grave,
To rest among the true and brave,
In holy ground, where yew-trees wave :

" Where, from church-windows sculptured fair,
Float out upon the evening air
The note of praise, the voice of prayer :

" Where no vain marble mockery
Insults with loud and boastful lie
The simple soldier's memory :

" Where sometimes little children go,
And read, in whisper'd accent slow,
The name of him who sleeps below."

Her voice died out : like one in dreams she sat.
" Alas ! " she sighed.   " For what can Woman do ?
Her life is aimless, and her death unknown :
Hemmed in by social forms she pines in vain.
Man has his work, but what can Woman do ? "
    And answer came there from the creeping gloom,
The creeping gloom that settled into night :
" Peace !   For thy lot is other than a man's :
His is a path of thorns : he beats them down :
He faces death : he wrestles with despair.
Thine is of roses, to adorn and cheer

The Path of Roses

His lonely life, and hide the thorns in flowers."
   She spake again : in bitter tone she spake :
" Aye, as a toy, the puppet of an hour,
Or a fair posy, newly plucked at morn,
But flung aside and withered ere the night."
   And answer came there from the creeping gloom,
The creeping gloom that blackened into night :
" So shalt thou be the lamp to light his path,
What time the shades of sorrow close around."
   And, so it seemed to her, an awful light
Pierced slowly through the darkness, orbed, and grew,
Until all passed away—the ancient room—
The sunlight dying through the trellised vine—
The one tall window—all had passed away,
And she was standing on the mighty hills.
   Beneath, around, and far as eye could see,
Squadron on squadron, stretched opposing hosts,
Ranked as for battle, mute and motionless.
Anon a distant thunder shook the ground,
The tramp of horses, and a troop shot by—
Plunged headlong in that living sea of men—
Plunged to their death : back from that fatal field
A scattered handful, fighting hard for life,
Broke through the serried lines ; but, as she gazed,
They shrank and melted, and their forms grew thin—
Grew pale as ghosts when the first morning ray
Dawns from the East—the trumpet's brazen blare
Died into silence—and the vision passed—
Passed to a room where sick and dying lay
In long, sad line—there brooded Fear and Pain—
Darkness was there, the shade of Azrael's wing.
But there was one that ever, to and fro,
Moved with light footfall : purely calm her face,

The Path of Roses

And those deep steadfast eyes that starred the gloom :
Still, as she went, she ministered to each
Comfort and counsel ; cooled the fevered brow
With softest touch, and in the listening ear
Of the pale sufferer whispered words of peace.
The dying warrior, gazing as she passed,
Clasped his thin hands and blessed her.   Bless her too,
Thou, who didst bless the merciful of old !
    So prayed the Lady, watching tearfully
Her gentle moving onward, till the night
Had veiled her wholly, and the vision passed.
    Then once again the solemn whisper came :
" So in the darkest path of man's despair,
Where War and Terror shake the troubled earth,
Lies woman's mission ; with unblenching brow
To pass through scenes of horror and affright
Where men grow sick and tremble : unto her
All things are sanctified, for all are good.
Nothing so mean, but shall deserve her care :
Nothing so great, but she may bear her part.
No life is vain : each hath his place assigned :
Do thou thy task, and leave the rest to God."
And there was silence, but the Lady made
No answer, save one deeply-breathed " Amen."
    And she arose, and in that darkening room
Stood lonely as a spirit of the night—
Stood calm and fearless in the gathered night—
And raised her eyes to heaven.   There were tears
Upon her face, but in her heart was peace,
Peace that the world nor gives nor takes away !

April 10, 1856.

THE VALLEY OF THE SHADOW OF DEATH

HARK, *said the dying man, and sighed,*
  To that complaining tone—
Like sprite condemned, each eventide,
  To walk the world alone.
At sunset, when the air is still,
I hear it creep from yonder hill :
It breathes upon me, dead and chill,
  A moment, and is gone.

My son, it minds me of a day
  Left half a life behind,
That I have prayed to put away
  For ever from my mind.
But bitter memory will not die :
It haunts my soul when none is nigh :
I hear its whisper in the sigh
  Of that complaining wind.

And now in death my soul is fain
  To tell the tale of fear
That hidden in my breast hath lain
  Through many a weary year :
Yet time would fail to utter all—
The evil spells that held me thrall,

412

The Valley of the Shadow of Death

And thrust my life from fall to fall,
   Thou needest not to hear.

The spells that bound me with a chain,
   Sin's stern behests to do,
Till Pleasure's self, invoked in vain,
   A heavy burden grew—
Till from my spirit's fevered eye,
A hunted thing, I seemed to fly
Through the dark woods that underlie
   Yon mountain-range of blue.

Deep in those woods I found a vale
   No sunlight visiteth,
Nor star, nor wandering moonbeam pale ;
   Where never comes the breath
Of summer-breeze—there in mine ear,
Even as I lingered half in fear,
I heard a whisper, cold and clear,
   " That is the gate of Death.

" O bitter is it to abide
   In weariness alway :
At dawn to sigh for eventide,
   At eventide for day.
Thy noon hath fled : thy sun hath shone :
The brightness of thy day is gone :
What need to lag and linger on
   Till life be cold and gray ?

" O well," it said, " beneath yon pool,
   In some still cavern deep,
The fevered brain might slumber cool,
   The eyes forget to weep :

The Valley of the Shadow of Death

Within that goblet's mystic rim
Are draughts of healing, stored for him
Whose heart is sick, whose sight is dim,
   Who prayeth but to sleep ! "

The evening-breeze went moaning by,
   Like mourner for the dead,
And stirred, with shrill complaining sigh,
   The tree-tops overhead :
My guardian-angel seemed to stand
And mutely wave a warning hand—
With sudden terror all unmanned,
   I turned myself and fled !

A cottage-gate stood open wide :
   Soft fell the dying ray
On two fair children, side by side,
   That rested from their play—
Together bent the earnest head,
As ever and anon they read
From one dear Book : the words they said
   Come back to me to-day.

Like twin cascades on mountain-stair
   Together wandered down
The ripples of the golden hair,
   The ripples of the brown :
While, through the tangled silken haze,
Blue eyes looked forth in eager gaze,
More starlike than the gems that blaze
   About a monarch's crown.

My son, there comes to each an hour
   When sinks the spirit's pride—

414

The Valley of the Shadow of Death

When weary hands forget their power
   The strokes of death to guide :
In such a moment, warriors say,
A word the panic-rout may stay,
A sudden charge redeem the day
   And turn the living tide.

I could not see, for blinding tears,
   The glories of the west :
A heavenly music filled mine ears,
   A heavenly peace my breast.
" Come unto Me, come unto Me—
All ye that labour, unto Me—
Ye heavy-laden, come to Me—
   And I will give you rest."

The night drew onwards : thin and blue
   The evening mists arise
To bathe the thirsty land in dew,
   As erst in Paradise—
While, over silent field and town,
The deep blue vault of heaven looked down ;
Not, as of old, in angry frown,
   But bright with angels' eyes.

Blest day ! Then first I heard the voice
   That since hath oft beguiled
These eyes from tears, and bid rejoice
   This heart with anguish wild—
Thy mother, boy, thou hast not known ;
So soon she left me here to moan—
Left me to weep and watch, alone,
   Our one beloved child.

The Valley of the Shadow of Death

Though, parted from my aching sight,
  Like homeward-speeding dove,
She passed into the perfect light
  That floods the world above ;
Yet our twin spirits, well I know—
Though one abide in pain below—
Love, as in summers long ago,
  And evermore shall love.

So with a glad and patient heart
  I move toward mine end :
The streams, that flow awhile apart,
  Shall both in ocean blend.
I dare not weep : I can but bless
The Love that pitied my distress,
And lent me, in Life's wilderness,
  So sweet and true a friend.

But if there be—O if there be
  A truth in what they say,
That angel-forms we cannot see
  Go with us on our way ;
Then surely she is with me here,
I dimly feel her spirit near—
The morning-mists grow thin and clear,
  And Death brings in the Day.

April 1868.

SOLITUDE

I LOVE the stillness of the wood :
   I love the music of the rill :
I love to couch in pensive mood
   Upon some silent hill.

Scarce heard, beneath yon arching trees,
   The silver-crested ripples pass ;
And, like a mimic brook, the breeze
   Whispers among the grass.

Here from the world I win release,
   Nor scorn of men, nor footstep rude,
Break in to mar the holy peace
   Of this great solitude.

Here may the silent tears I weep
   Lull the vexed spirit into rest,
As infants sob themselves to sleep
   Upon a mother's breast.

But when the bitter hour is gone,
   And the keen throbbing pangs are still,
Oh, sweetest then to couch alone
   Upon some silent hill !

To live in joys that once have been,
   To put the cold world out of sight,

Solitude

And deck life's drear and barren scene
   With hues of rainbow-light.

For what to man the gift of breath,
   If sorrow be his lot below ;
If all the day that ends in death
   Be dark with clouds of woe ?

Shall the poor transport of an hour
   Repay long years of sore distress—
The fragrance of a lonely flower
   Make glad the wilderness ?

Ye golden hours of Life's young spring,
   Of innocence, of love and truth !
Bright, beyond all imagining,
   Thou fairy-dream of youth !

I'd give all wealth that years have piled,
   The slow result of Life's decay,
To be once more a little child
   For one bright summer-day.

March 16, 1853.

BEATRICE

In her eyes is the living light
   Of a wanderer to earth
From a far celestial height :
   Summers five are all the span—
   Summers five since Time began
To veil in mists of human night
   A shining angel-birth.

Does an angel look from her eyes ?
   Will she suddenly spring away,
And soar to her home in the skies ?
   Beatrice ! Blessing and blessed to be !
   Beatrice ! Still, as I gaze on thee,
Visions of two sweet maids arise,
   Whose life was of yesterday :

Of a Beatrice pale and stern,
   With the lips of a dumb despair,
With the innocent eyes that yearn—
   Yearn for the young sweet hours of life,
   Far from sorrow and far from strife,
For the happy summers, that never return,
   When the world seemed good and fair :

Of a Beatrice glorious, bright—
   Of a sainted, ethereal maid,

Beatrice

Whose blue eyes are deep fountains of light,
　　Cheering the poet that broodeth apart,
　　Filling with gladness his desolate heart,
Like the moon when she shines thro' a cloudless
　　night
　　On a world of silence and shade.

And the visions waver and faint,
　　And the visions vanish away
That my fancy delighted to paint—
　　She is here at my side, a living child,
　　With the glowing cheek and the tresses wild,
Nor death-pale martyr, nor radiant saint,
　　Yet stainless and bright as they.

For I think, if a grim wild beast
　　Were to come from his charnel-cave,
From his jungle-home in the East—
　　Stealthily creeping with bated breath,
　　Stealthily creeping with eyes of death—
He would all forget his dream of the feast,
　　And crouch at her feet a slave.

She would twine her hand in his mane :
　　She would prattle in silvery tone,
Like the tinkle of summer-rain—
　　Questioning him with her laughing eyes,
　　Questioning him with a glad surprise,
Till she caught from those fierce eyes again
　　The love that lit her own.

And be sure, if a savage heart,
　　In a mask of human guise,

Beatrice

Were to come on her here apart—
    Bound for a dark and a deadly deed,
    Hurrying past with pitiless speed—
He would suddenly falter and guiltily start
    At the glance of her pure blue eyes.

Nay, be sure, if an angel fair,
    A bright seraph undefiled,
Were to stoop from the trackless air,
    Fain would she linger in glad amaze—
    Lovingly linger to ponder and gaze,
With a sister's love and a sister's care,
    On the happy, innocent child.

Dec. 4, 1862.

STOLEN WATERS

The light was faint, and soft the air
   That breathed around the place ;
And she was lithe, and tall, and fair,
   And with a wayward grace
   Her queenly head she bare.

With glowing cheek, with gleaming eye,
   She met me on the way :
My spirit owned the witchery
   Within her smile that lay :
I followed her, I knew not why.

The trees were thick with many a fruit,
   The grass with many a flower :
My soul was dead, my tongue was mute,
   In that accursèd hour.

And, in my dream, with silvery voice,
   She said, or seemed to say,
" Youth is the season to rejoice—"
   I could not choose but stay :
   I could not say her nay.

She plucked a branch above her head,
   With rarest fruitage laden :
" Drink of the juice, Sir Knight," she said :
   " 'Tis good for knight and maiden."

Stolen Waters

Oh, blind mine eye that would not trace—
　　Oh, deaf mine ear that would not heed—
The mocking smile upon her face,
　　The mocking voice of greed !

I drank the juice ; and straightway felt
　　A fire within my brain :
My soul within me seemed to melt
　　In sweet delirious pain.

" Sweet is the stolen draught," she said :
　　" Hath sweetness stint or measure ?
Pleasant the secret hoard of bread :
　　What bars us from our pleasure ? "

" Yea, take we pleasure while we may,"
　　I heard myself replying.
In the red sunset, far away,
　　My happier life was dying :
My heart was sad, my voice was gay.

And unawares, I knew not how,
　　I kissed her dainty finger-tips,
I kissed her on the lily brow,
　　I kissed her on the false, false lips—
That burning kiss, I feel it now !

" True love gives true love of the best :
　　Then take," I cried, " my heart to thee ! "
The very heart from out my breast
　　I plucked, I gave it willingly :
　　Her very heart she gave to me—
Then died the glory from the west.

Stolen Waters

In the gray light I saw her face,
  And it was withered, old, and gray ;
The flowers were fading in their place,
  Were fading with the fading day.

Forth from her, like a hunted deer,
  Through all that ghastly night I fled,
And still behind me seemed to hear
  Her fierce unflagging tread ;
And scarce drew breath for fear.

Yet marked I well how strangely seemed
  The heart within my breast to sleep :
Silent it lay, or so I dreamed,
  With never a throb or leap.

For hers was now my heart, she said,
  The heart that once had been mine own :
And in my breast I bore instead
  A cold, cold heart of stone.
So grew the morning overhead.

The sun shot downward through the trees
  His old familiar flame :
All ancient sounds upon the breeze
  From copse and meadow came—
  But I was not the same.

They call me mad : I smile, I weep,
  Uncaring how or why :
Yea, when one's heart is laid asleep,
  What better than to die ?
So that the grave be dark and deep.

Stolen Waters

To die ! To die ? And yet, methinks,
  I drink of life, to-day,
Deep as the thirsty traveller drinks
  Of fountain by the way :
My voice is sad, my heart is gay.

When yestereve was on the wane,
  I heard a clear voice singing
So sweetly that, like summer-rain,
  My happy tears came springing :
My human heart returned again.

  " *A rosy child,*
Sitting and singing, in a garden fair,
    The joy of hearing, seeing,
    The simple joy of being—
Or twining rosebuds in the golden hair
    That ripples free and wild.

    " *A sweet pale child—*
Wearily looking to the purple West—
    Waiting the great For-ever
    That suddenly shall sever
The cruel chains that hold her from her rest—
    By earth-joys unbeguiled.

    " *An angel-child—*
Gazing with living eyes on a dead face :
    The mortal form forsaken,
    That none may now awaken,
That lieth painless, moveless in her place,
    As though in death she smiled !

Stolen Waters

" Be as a child—
So shalt thou sing for very joy of breath—
So shalt thou wait thy dying,
In holy transport lying—
So pass rejoicing through the gate of death,
In garment undefiled."

Then call me what they will, I know
   That now my soul is glad :
If this be madness, better so,
   Far better to be mad,
Weeping or smiling as I go.

For if I weep, it is that now
   I see how deep a loss is mine,
And feel how brightly round my brow
   The coronal might shine,
Had I but kept mine early vow :

And if I smile, it is that now
   I see the promise of the years—
The garland waiting for my brow,
   That must be won with tears,
With pain—with death—I care not how.

May 9, 1862.

THE WILLOW-TREE

THE morn was bright, the steeds were light,
  The wedding guests were gay :
Young Ellen stood within the wood
  And watched them pass away.
She scarcely saw the gallant train :
  The tear-drop dimmed her e'e :
Unheard the maiden did complain
  Beneath the Willow-Tree.

" Oh, Robin, thou didst love me well,
  Till, on a bitter day,
She came, the Lady Isabel,
  And stole thy heart away.
My tears are vain : I live again
  In days that used to be,
When I could meet thy welcome feet
  Beneath the Willow-Tree.

" Oh, Willow gray, I may not stay
  Till Spring renew thy leaf ;
But I will hide myself away,
  And nurse a lonely grief.
It shall not dim Life's joy for him :
  My tears he shall not see :

The Willow-Tree

While he is by, I'll come not nigh
　　My weeping Willow-Tree.

" But when I die, oh, let me lie
　　Beneath thy loving shade,
That he may loiter careless by,
　　Where I am lowly laid.
And let the white white marble tell,
　　If he should stoop to see,
' Here lies a maid that loved thee well,
　　Beneath the Willow-Tree.' "

1859.

ONLY A WOMAN'S HAIR

["After the death of Dean Swift, there was found among his papers a small packet containing a single lock of hair and inscribed with the above words."]

" ONLY a woman's hair ! "   Fling it aside !
    A bubble on Life's mighty stream :
Heed it not, man, but watch the broadening tide
    Bright with the western beam.

Nay !   In those words there rings from other years
    The echo of a long low cry,
Where a proud spirit wrestles with its tears
    In loneliest agony.

And, as I touch that lock, strange visions throng
    Upon my soul with dreamy grace—
Of woman's hair, the theme of poet's song
    In every time and place.

A child's bright tresses, by the breezes kissed
    To sweet disorder as she flies,
Veiling, beneath a cloud of golden mist,
    Flushed cheek and laughing eyes—

Or fringing, like a shadow, raven-black,
    The glory of a queen-like face—

429

Only a Woman's Hair

Or from a gipsy's sunny brow tossed back
　　In wild and wanton grace——

Or crown-like on the hoary head of Age,
　　Whose tale of life is well-nigh told—
Or, last, in dreams I make my pilgrimage
　　To Bethany of old.

I see the feast—the purple and the gold ;
　　The gathering crowd of Pharisees,
Whose scornful eyes are centred to behold
　　Yon woman on her knees.

The stifled sob rings strangely on mine ears,
　　Wrung from the depth of sin's despair :
And still she bathes the sacred feet with tears,
　　And wipes them with her hair.

He scorned not then the simple loving deed
　　Of her, the lowest and the last ;
Then scorn not thou, but use with earnest heed
　　This relic of the past.

The eyes that loved it once no longer wake :
　　So lay it by with reverent care—
Touching it tenderly for sorrow's sake—
　　It is a woman's hair.

Feb. 17, 1862.

THE SAILOR'S WIFE

SEE ! There are tears upon her face—
  Tears newly shed, and scarcely dried :
Close, in an agonised embrace,
  She clasps the infant at her side.

Peace dwells in those soft-lidded eyes,
  Those parted lips that faintly smile—
Peace, the foretaste of Paradise,
  In heart too young for care or guile.

No peace that mother's features wear ;
  But quivering lip, and knotted brow,
And broken mutterings, all declare
  The fearful dream that haunts her now.

The storm-wind, rushing through the sky,
  Wails from the depths of cloudy space ;
Shrill, piercing as the seaman's cry
  When death and he are face to face.

Familiar tones are in the gale :
  They ring upon her startled ear :
And quick and low she pants the tale
  That tells of agony and fear :

The Sailor's Wife

" Still that phantom-ship is nigh—
   With a vexed and life-like motion,
All beneath an angry sky,
   Rocking on an angry ocean.

" Round the straining mast and shrouds
   Throng the spirits of the storm :
Darkly seen through driving clouds,
   Bends each gaunt and ghastly form.

" See !   The good ship yields at last !
   Dumbly yields, and fights no more ;
Driving, in the frantic blast,
   Headlong on the fatal shore.

" Hark !   I hear her battered side,
   With a low and sullen shock,
Dashed, amid the foaming tide,
   Full upon a sunken rock.

" His face shines out against the sky,
   Like a ghost, so cold and white ;
With a dead despairing eye
   Gazing through the gathered night.

" Is he watching, through the dark,
   Where a mocking ghostly hand
Points a faint and feeble spark
   Glimmering from the distant land ?

" Sees he, in this hour of dread,
   Hearth and home and wife and child ?
Loved ones who, in summers fled,
   Clung to him and wept and smiled ?

The Sailor's Wife

" Reeling sinks the fated bark
  To her tomb beneath the wave :
Must he perish in the dark—
  Not a hand stretched out to save ?

" See the spirits, how they crowd !
  Watching death with eyes that burn !
Waves rush in——" she shrieks aloud,
  Ere her waking sense return.

The storm is gone : the skies are clear :
  Hush'd is that bitter cry of pain :
The only sound, that meets her ear,
  The heaving of the sullen main.

Though heaviness endure the night,
  Yet joy shall come with break of day :
She shudders with a strange delight—
  The fearful dream is pass'd away.

She wakes : the gray dawn streaks the dark :
  With early song the copses ring :
Far off she hears the watch-dog bark
  A joyful bark of welcoming !

Feb. 23, 1857.

AFTER THREE DAYS

["Written after seeing Holman Hunt's picture,
The Finding of Christ in the Temple."]

    I STOOD within the gate
Of a great temple, 'mid the living stream
Of worshippers that thronged its regal state
    Fair-pictured in my dream.

    Jewels and gold were there ;
And floors of marble lent a crystal sheen
To body forth, as in a lower air,
    The wonders of the scene.

    Such wild and lavish grace
Had whispers in it of a coming doom ;
As richest flowers lie strown about the face
    Of her that waits the tomb.

    The wisest of the land
Had gathered there, three solemn trysting-days,
For high debate : men stood on either hand
    To listen and to gaze.

    The aged brows were bent,
Bent to a frown, half thought, and half annoy,
That all their stores of subtlest argument
    Were baffled by a boy.

After Three Days

In each averted face
I marked but scorn and loathing, till mine eyes
Fell upon one that stirred not in his place,
    Tranced in a dumb surprise.

Surely within his mind
Strange thoughts are born, until he doubts the lore
Of those old men, blind leaders of the blind,
    Whose kingdom is no more.

Surely he sees afar
A day of death the stormy future brings ;
The crimson setting of the. herald-star
    That led the Eastern kings.

Thus, as a sunless deep
Mirrors the shining heights that crown the bay,
So did my soul create anew in sleep
    The picture seen by day.

Gazers came and went—
A restless hum of voices marked the spot—
In varying shades of critic discontent
    Prating they knew not what.

" Where is the comely limb,
The form attuned in every perfect part,
The beauty that we should desire in him ? "
    Ah ! Fools and slow of heart !

Look into those deep eyes,
Deep as the grave, and strong with love divine ;
Those tender, pure, and fathomless mysteries,
    That seem to pierce through thine.

After Three Days

Look into those deep eyes,
Stirred to unrest by breath of coming strife,
Until a longing in thy soul arise
   That this indeed were life :

That thou couldst find Him there,
Bend at His sacred feet thy willing knee,
And from thy heart pour out the passionate prayer,
   " Lord, let me follow Thee ! "

But see the crowd divide :
Mother and sire have found their lost one now :
The gentle voice, that fain would seem to chide,
   Whispers, " Son, why hast thou "—

In tone of sad amaze—
" Thus dealt with us, that art our dearest thing ?
Behold, thy sire and I, three weary days,
   Have sought thee sorrowing."

And I had stayed to hear
The loving words, "How is it that ye sought ?"—
But that the sudden lark, with matins clear,
   Severed the links of thought.

Then over all there fell
Shadow and silence ; and my dream was fled,
As fade the phantoms of a wizard's cell
   When the dark charm is said.

Yet, in the gathering light,
I lay with half-shut eyes that would not wake,
Lovingly clinging to the skirts of night
   For that sweet vision's sake.

Feb. 16, 1861.

FACES IN THE FIRE

THE night creeps onward, sad and slow :
In these red embers' dying glow
The forms of Fancy come and go.

An island-farm—broad seas of corn
Stirred by the wandering breath of morn—
The happy spot where I was born.

The picture fadeth in its place :
Amid the glow I seem to trace
The shifting semblance of a face.

'Tis now a little childish form—
Red lips for kisses pouted warm—
And elf-locks tangled in the storm.

'Tis now a grave and gentle maid,
At her own beauty half afraid,
Shrinking, and willing to be stayed.

Oh, Time was young, and Life was warm,
When first I saw that fairy-form,
Her dark hair tossing in the storm.

And fast and free these pulses played,
When last I met that gentle maid—
When last her hand in mine was laid.

437

Faces in the Fire

Those locks of jet are turned to gray,
And she is strange and far away
That might have been mine own to-day—

That might have been mine own, my dear,
Through many and many a happy year—
That might have sat beside me here.

Ay, changeless through the changing scene,
The ghostly whisper rings between,
The dark refrain of " might have been."

The race is o'er I might have run :
The deeds are past I might have done ;
And sere the wreath I might have won.

Sunk is the last faint flickering blaze :
The vision of departed days
Is vanished even as I gaze.

The pictures, with their ruddy light,
Are changed to dust and ashes white,
And I am left alone with night.

Jan. 1860.

A LESSON IN LATIN

OUR Latin books, in motley row,
    Invite us to our task—
Gay Horace, stately Cicero :
Yet there's one verb, when once we know,
    No higher skill we ask :
This ranks all other lore above—
We've learned " ' *Amare* ' means ' *to love* ' *!* "

So, hour by hour, from flower to flower,
    We sip the sweets of Life :
Till, all too soon, the clouds arise,
And flaming cheeks and flashing eyes
    Proclaim the dawn of strife :
With half a smile and half a sigh,
" *Amare !*   *Bitter One !* " we cry.

Last night we owned, with looks forlorn,
    " Too well the scholar knows
There is no rose without a thorn "—
But peace is made !   We sing, this morn,
    " No thorn without a rose ! "
Our Latin lesson is complete :
We've learned that Love is Bitter-Sweet !

May 1888.

439

PUCK LOST AND FOUND

[" Inscribed in two books . . . presented to a little girl and boy, as a sort of memento of a visit paid by them to the author one day, on which occasion he taught them the pastime of folding paper ' pistols.' "]

PUCK has fled the haunts of men :
　　Ridicule has made him wary :
In the woods, and down the glen,
　　No one meets a Fairy !

" Cream ! " the greedy Goblin cries—
　　Empties the deserted dairy—
Steals the spoons, and off he flies.
　　Still we seek our Fairy !

Ah !　What form is entering ?
　　Lovelit eyes and laughter airy !
Is not this a better thing,
Child, whose visit thus I sing,
　　Even than a Fairy ?

Nov. 22, 1891.

440

Puck Lost and Found

PUCK has ventured back agen :
   Ridicule no more affrights him :
In the very haunts of men
   Newer sport delights him.

Capering lightly to and fro,
   Ever frolicking and funning—
" Crack ! " the mimic pistols go !
   Hark ! The noise is stunning !

All too soon will Childhood gay
   Realise Life's sober sadness.
Let's be merry while we may,
Innocent and happy Fay !
   Elves were made for gladness !

Nov. 25, 1891.

INDEX TO FIRST LINES.

Index to First Lines

444

Index to First Lines

445

Index to First Lines

A CATALOGUE OF SELECTED DOVER BOOKS
IN ALL FIELDS OF INTEREST

A CATALOGUE OF SELECTED DOVER
BOOKS IN ALL FIELDS OF INTEREST

RACKHAM'S COLOR ILLUSTRATIONS FOR WAGNER'S RING. Rackham's finest mature work—all 64 full-color watercolors in a faithful and lush interpretation of the *Ring*. Full-sized plates on coated stock of the paintings used by opera companies for authentic staging of Wagner. Captions aid in following complete Ring cycle. Introduction. 64 illustrations plus vignettes. 72pp. 8⅝ x 11¼.   23779-6 Pa. $6.00

CONTEMPORARY POLISH POSTERS IN FULL COLOR, edited by Joseph Czestochowski. 46 full-color examples of brilliant school of Polish graphic design, selected from world's first museum (near Warsaw) dedicated to poster art. Posters on circuses, films, plays, concerts all show cosmopolitan influences, free imagination. Introduction. 48pp. 9⅜ x 12¼.   23780-X Pa. $6.00

GRAPHIC WORKS OF EDVARD MUNCH, Edvard Munch. 90 haunting, evocative prints by first major Expressionist artist and one of the greatest graphic artists of his time: *The Scream, Anxiety, Death Chamber, The Kiss, Madonna,* etc. Introduction by Alfred Werner. 90pp. 9 x 12.   23765-6 Pa. $5.00

THE GOLDEN AGE OF THE POSTER, Hayward and Blanche Cirker. 70 extraordinary posters in full colors, from Maitres de l'Affiche, Mucha, Lautrec, Bradley, Cheret, Beardsley, many others. Total of 78pp. 9⅜ x 12¼.   22753-7 Pa. $5.95

THE NOTEBOOKS OF LEONARDO DA VINCI, edited by J. P. Richter. Extracts from manuscripts reveal great genius; on painting, sculpture, anatomy, sciences, geography, etc. Both Italian and English. 186 ms. pages reproduced, plus 500 additional drawings, including studies for *Last Supper*, Sforza monument, etc. 860pp. 7⅞ x 10¾. (Available in U.S. only)   22572-0, 22573-9 Pa., Two-vol. set $15.90

THE CODEX NUTTALL, as first edited by Zelia Nuttall. Only inexpensive edition, in full color, of a pre-Columbian Mexican (Mixtec) book. 88 color plates show kings, gods, heroes, temples, sacrifices. New explanatory, historical introduction by Arthur G. Miller. 96pp. 11⅜ x 8½. (Available in U.S. only)   23168-2 Pa. $7.95

UNE SEMAINE DE BONTÉ, A SURREALISTIC NOVEL IN COLLAGE, Max Ernst. Masterpiece created out of 19th-century periodical illustrations, explores worlds of terror and surprise. Some consider this Ernst's greatest work. 208pp. 8⅛ x 11.   23252-2 Pa. $6.00

AN AUTOBIOGRAPHY, Margaret Sanger. Exciting personal account of hard-fought battle for woman's right to birth control, against prejudice, church, law. Foremost feminist document. 504pp. 5⅜ x 8½.
20470-7 Pa. $5.50

MY BONDAGE AND MY FREEDOM, Frederick Douglass. Born as a slave, Douglass became outspoken force in antislavery movement. The best of Douglass's autobiographies. Graphic description of slave life. Introduction by P. Foner. 464pp. 5⅜ x 8½.
22457-0 Pa. $5.50

LIVING MY LIFE, Emma Goldman. Candid, no holds barred account by foremost American anarchist: her own life, anarchist movement, famous contemporaries, ideas and their impact. Struggles and confrontations in America, plus deportation to U.S.S.R. Shocking inside account of persecution of anarchists under Lenin. 13 plates. Total of 944pp. 5⅜ x 8½.
22543-7, 22544-5 Pa., Two-vol. set $12.00

LETTERS AND NOTES ON THE MANNERS, CUSTOMS AND CONDITIONS OF THE NORTH AMERICAN INDIANS, George Catlin. Classic account of life among Plains Indians: ceremonies, hunt, warfare, etc. Dover edition reproduces for first time all original paintings. 312 plates. 572pp. of text. 6⅛ x 9¼.
22118-0, 22119-9 Pa.. Two-vol. set $12.00

THE MAYA AND THEIR NEIGHBORS, edited by Clarence L. Hay, others. Synoptic view of Maya civilization in broadest sense, together with Northern, Southern neighbors. Integrates much background, valuable detail not elsewhere. Prepared by greatest scholars: Kroeber, Morley, Thompson, Spinden, Vaillant, many others. Sometimes called Tozzer Memorial Volume. 60 illustrations, linguistic map. 634pp. 5⅜ x 8½.
23510-6 Pa. $10.00

HANDBOOK OF THE INDIANS OF CALIFORNIA, A. L. Kroeber. Foremost American anthropologist offers complete ethnographic study of each group. Monumental classic. 459 illustrations, maps. 995pp. 5⅜ x 8½.
23368-5 Pa. $13.00

SHAKTI AND SHAKTA, Arthur Avalon. First book to give clear, cohesive analysis of Shakta doctrine, Shakta ritual and Kundalini Shakti (yoga). Important work by one of world's foremost students of Shaktic and Tantric thought. 732pp. 5⅜ x 8½. (Available in U.S. only)
23645-5 Pa. $7.95

AN INTRODUCTION TO THE STUDY OF THE MAYA HIEROGLYPHS, Syvanus Griswold Morley. Classic study by one of the truly great figures in hieroglyph research. Still the best introduction for the student for reading Maya hieroglyphs. New introduction by J. Eric S. Thompson. 117 illustrations. 284pp. 5⅜ x 8½.
23108-9 Pa. $4.00

A STUDY OF MAYA ART, Herbert J. Spinden. Landmark classic interprets Maya symbolism, estimates styles, covers ceramics, architecture, murals, stone carvings as artforms. Still a basic book in area. New introduction by J. Eric Thompson. Over 750 illustrations. 341pp. 8⅜ x 11¼.
21235-1 Pa. $6.95

HOUSEHOLD STORIES BY THE BROTHERS GRIMM. All the great Grimm stories: "Rumpelstiltskin," "Snow White," "Hansel and Gretel," etc., with 114 illustrations by Walter Crane. 269pp. 5⅜ x 8½.
21080-4 Pa. $3.50

SLEEPING BEAUTY, illustrated by Arthur Rackham. Perhaps the fullest, most delightful version ever, told by C. S. Evans. Rackham's best work. 49 illustrations. 110pp. 7⅞ x 10¾. 22756-1 Pa. $2.50

AMERICAN FAIRY TALES, L. Frank Baum. Young cowboy lassoes Father Time; dummy in Mr. Floman's department store window comes to life; and 10 other fairy tales. 41 illustrations by N. P. Hall, Harry Kennedy, Ike Morgan, and Ralph Gardner. 209pp. 5⅜ x 8½. 23643-9 Pa. $3.00

THE WONDERFUL WIZARD OF OZ, L. Frank Baum. Facsimile in full color of America's finest children's classic. Introduction by Martin Gardner. 143 illustrations by W. W. Denslow. 267pp. 5⅜ x 8½.
20691-2 Pa. $3.50

THE TALE OF PETER RABBIT, Beatrix Potter. The inimitable Peter's terrifying adventure in Mr. McGregor's garden, with all 27 wonderful, full-color Potter illustrations. 55pp. 4¼ x 5½. (Available in U.S. only)
22827-4 Pa. $1.25

THE STORY OF KING ARTHUR AND HIS KNIGHTS, Howard Pyle. Finest children's version of life of King Arthur. 48 illustrations by Pyle. 131pp. 6⅛ x 9¼. 21445-1 Pa. $4.95

CARUSO'S CARICATURES, Enrico Caruso. Great tenor's remarkable caricatures of self, fellow musicians, composers, others. Toscanini, Puccini, Farrar, etc. Impish, cutting, insightful. 473 illustrations. Preface by M. Sisca. 217pp. 8⅜ x 11¼. 23528-9 Pa. $6.95

PERSONAL NARRATIVE OF A PILGRIMAGE TO ALMADINAH AND MECCAH, Richard Burton. Great travel classic by remarkably colorful personality. Burton, disguised as a Moroccan, visited sacred shrines of Islam, narrowly escaping death. Wonderful observations of Islamic life, customs, personalities. 47 illustrations. Total of 959pp. 5⅜ x 8½.
21217-3, 21218-1 Pa., Two-vol. set $12.00

INCIDENTS OF TRAVEL IN YUCATAN, John L. Stephens. Classic (1843) exploration of jungles of Yucatan, looking for evidences of Maya civilization. Travel adventures, Mexican and Indian culture, etc. Total of 669pp. 5⅜ x 8½. 20926-1, 20927-X Pa., Two-vol. set $7.90

AMERICAN LITERARY AUTOGRAPHS FROM WASHINGTON IRVING TO HENRY JAMES, Herbert Cahoon, et al. Letters, poems, manuscripts of Hawthorne, Thoreau, Twain, Alcott, Whitman, 67 other prominent American authors. Reproductions, full transcripts and commentary. Plus checklist of all American Literary Autographs in The Pierpont Morgan Library. Printed on exceptionally high-quality paper. 136 illustrations. 212pp. 9⅛ x 12¼. 23548-3 Pa. $12.50

UNCLE SILAS, J. Sheridan LeFanu. Victorian Gothic mystery novel, considered by many best of period, even better than Collins or Dickens. Wonderful psychological terror. Introduction by Frederick Shroyer. 436pp. 5⅜ x 8½. 21715-9 Pa. $6.00

JURGEN, James Branch Cabell. The great erotic fantasy of the 1920's that delighted thousands, shocked thousands more. Full final text, Lane edition with 13 plates by Frank Pape. 346pp. 5⅜ x 8½. 23507-6 Pa. $4.50

THE CLAVERINGS, Anthony Trollope. Major novel, chronicling aspects of British Victorian society, personalities. Reprint of Cornhill serialization, 16 plates by M. Edwards; first reprint of full text. Introduction by Norman Donaldson. 412pp. 5⅜ x 8½. 23464-9 Pa. $5.00

KEPT IN THE DARK, Anthony Trollope. Unusual short novel about Victorian morality and abnormal psychology by the great English author. Probably the first American publication. Frontispiece by Sir John Millais. 92pp. 6½ x 9¼. 23609-9 Pa. $2.50

RALPH THE HEIR, Anthony Trollope. Forgotten tale of illegitimacy, inheritance. Master novel of Trollope's later years. Victorian country estates, clubs, Parliament, fox hunting, world of fully realized characters. Reprint of 1871 edition. 12 illustrations by F. A. Faser. 434pp. of text. 5⅜ x 8½. 23642-0 Pa. $5.00

YEKL and THE IMPORTED BRIDEGROOM AND OTHER STORIES OF THE NEW YORK GHETTO, Abraham Cahan. Film *Hester Street* based on *Yekl* (1896). Novel, other stories among first about Jewish immigrants of N.Y.'s East Side. Highly praised by W. D. Howells—Cahan "a new star of realism." New introduction by Bernard G. Richards. 240pp. 5⅜ x 8½. 22427-9 Pa. $3.50

THE HIGH PLACE, James Branch Cabell. Great fantasy writer's enchanting comedy of disenchantment set in 18th-century France. Considered by some critics to be even better than his famous *Jurgen*. 10 illustrations and numerous vignettes by noted fantasy artist Frank C. Pape. 320pp. 5⅜ x 8½. 23670-6 Pa. $4.00

ALICE'S ADVENTURES UNDER GROUND, Lewis Carroll. Facsimile of ms. Carroll gave Alice Liddell in 1864. Different in many ways from final Alice. Handlettered, illustrated by Carroll. Introduction by Martin Gardner. 128pp. 5⅜ x 8½. 21482-6 Pa. $2.50

FAVORITE ANDREW LANG FAIRY TALE BOOKS IN MANY COLORS, Andrew Lang. The four Lang favorites in a boxed set—the complete *Red, Green, Yellow* and *Blue* Fairy Books. 164 stories; 439 illustrations by Lancelot Speed, Henry Ford and G. P. Jacomb Hood. Total of about 1500pp. 5⅜ x 8½. 23407-X Boxed set, Pa. $15.95

A MAYA GRAMMAR, Alfred M. Tozzer. Practical, useful English-language grammar by the Harvard anthropologist who was one of the three greatest American scholars in the area of Maya culture. Phonetics, grammatical processes, syntax, more. 301pp. 5⅜ x 8½. 23465-7 Pa. $4.00

THE JOURNAL OF HENRY D. THOREAU, edited by Bradford Torrey, F. H. Allen. Complete reprinting of 14 volumes, 1837-61, over two million words; the sourcebooks for *Walden*, etc. Definitive. All original sketches, plus 75 photographs. Introduction by Walter Harding. Total of 1804pp. 8½ x 12¼. 20312-3, 20313-1 Clothbd., Two-vol. set $70.00

CLASSIC GHOST STORIES, Charles Dickens and others. 18 wonderful stories you've wanted to reread: "The Monkey's Paw," "The House and the Brain," "The Upper Berth," "The Signalman," "Dracula's Guest," "The Tapestried Chamber," etc. Dickens, Scott, Mary Shelley, Stoker, etc. 330pp. 5⅜ x 8½. 20735-8 Pa. $4.50

SEVEN SCIENCE FICTION NOVELS, H. G. Wells. Full novels. *First Men in the Moon, Island of Dr. Moreau, War of the Worlds, Food of the Gods, Invisible Man, Time Machine, In the Days of the Comet.* A basic science-fiction library. 1015pp. 5⅜ x 8½. (Available in U.S. only) 20264-X Clothbd. $8.95

ARMADALE, Wilkie Collins. Third great mystery novel by the author of *The Woman in White* and *The Moonstone*. Ingeniously plotted narrative shows an exceptional command of character, incident and mood. Original magazine version with 40 illustrations. 597pp. 5⅜ x 8½. 23429-0 Pa. $6.00

MASTERS OF MYSTERY, H. Douglas Thomson. The first book in English (1931) devoted to history and aesthetics of detective story. Poe, Doyle, LeFanu, Dickens, many others, up to 1930. New introduction and notes by E. F. Bleiler. 288pp. 5⅜ x 8½. (Available in U.S. only) 23606-4 Pa. $4.00

FLATLAND, E. A. Abbott. Science-fiction classic explores life of 2-D being in 3-D world. Read also as introduction to thought about hyperspace. Introduction by Banesh Hoffmann. 16 illustrations. 103pp. 5⅜ x 8½. 20001-9 Pa. $2.00

THREE SUPERNATURAL NOVELS OF THE VICTORIAN PERIOD, edited, with an introduction, by E. F. Bleiler. Reprinted complete and unabridged, three great classics of the supernatural: *The Haunted Hotel* by Wilkie Collins, *The Haunted House at Latchford* by Mrs. J. H. Riddell, and *The Lost Stradivarius* by J. Meade Falkner. 325pp. 5⅜ x 8½. 22571-2 Pa. $4.00

AYESHA: THE RETURN OF "SHE," H. Rider Haggard. Virtuoso sequel featuring the great mythic creation, Ayesha, in an adventure that is fully as good as the first book, *She*. Original magazine version, with 47 original illustrations by Maurice Greiffenhagen. 189pp. 6½ x 9¼. 23649-8 Pa. $3.50

PRINCIPLES OF ORCHESTRATION, Nikolay Rimsky-Korsakov. Great classical orchestrator provides fundamentals of tonal resonance, progression of parts, voice and orchestra, tutti effects, much else in major document. 330pp. of musical excerpts. 489pp. 6½ x 9¼.   21266-1 Pa. **$7.50**

TRISTAN UND ISOLDE, Richard Wagner. Full orchestral score with complete instrumentation. Do not confuse with piano reduction. Commentary by Felix Mottl, great Wagnerian conductor and scholar. Study score. 655pp. 8⅛ x 11.   22915-7 Pa. $13.95

REQUIEM IN FULL SCORE, Giuseppe Verdi. Immensely popular with choral groups and music lovers. Republication of edition published by C. F. Peters, Leipzig, n. d. German frontmaker in English translation. Glossary. Text in Latin. Study score. 204pp. 9⅜ x 12¼.
23682-X Pa. $6.00

COMPLETE CHAMBER MUSIC FOR STRINGS, Felix Mendelssohn. All of Mendelssohn's chamber music: Octet, 2 Quintets, 6 Quartets, and Four Pieces for String Quartet. (Nothing with piano is included). Complete works edition (1874-7). Study score. 283 pp. 9⅜ x 12¼.
23679-X Pa. **$7.50**

POPULAR SONGS OF NINETEENTH-CENTURY AMERICA, edited by Richard Jackson. 64 most important songs: "Old Oaken Bucket," "Arkansas Traveler," "Yellow Rose of Texas," etc. Authentic original sheet music, full introduction and commentaries. 290pp. 9 x 12.   23270-0 Pa. **$7.95**

COLLECTED PIANO WORKS, Scott Joplin. Edited by Vera Brodsky Lawrence. Practically all of Joplin's piano works—rags, two-steps, marches, waltzes, etc., 51 works in all. Extensive introduction by Rudi Blesh. Total of 345pp. 9 x 12.   23106-2 Pa. $14.95

BASIC PRINCIPLES OF CLASSICAL BALLET, Agrippina Vaganova. Great Russian theoretician, teacher explains methods for teaching classical ballet; incorporates best from French, Italian, Russian schools. 118 illustrations. 175pp. 5⅜ x 8½.   22036-2 Pa. $2.50

CHINESE CHARACTERS, L. Wieger. Rich analysis of 2300 characters according to traditional systems into primitives. Historical-semantic analysis to phonetics (Classical Mandarin) and radicals. 820pp. 6⅛ x 9¼.
21321-8 Pa. $10.00

EGYPTIAN LANGUAGE: EASY LESSONS IN EGYPTIAN HIERO-GLYPHICS, E. A. Wallis Budge. Foremost Egyptologist offers Egyptian grammar, explanation of hieroglyphics, many reading texts, dictionary of symbols. 246pp. 5 x 7½. (Available in U.S. only)
21394-3 Clothbd. $7.50

AN ETYMOLOGICAL DICTIONARY OF MODERN ENGLISH, Ernest Weekley. Richest, fullest work, by foremost British lexicographer. Detailed word histories. Inexhaustible. Do not confuse this with *Concise Etymological Dictionary,* which is abridged. Total of 856pp. 6½ x 9¼.
21873-2, 21874-0 Pa., Two-vol. set $12.00

HOLLYWOOD GLAMOUR PORTRAITS, edited by John Kobal. 145 photos capture the stars from 1926-49, the high point in portrait photography. Gable, Harlow, Bogart, Bacall, Hedy Lamarr, Marlene Dietrich, Robert Montgomery, Marlon Brando, Veronica Lake; 94 stars in all. Full background on photographers, technical aspects, much more. Total of 160pp. 8⅜ x 11¼.   23352-9 Pa. $6.00

THE NEW YORK STAGE: FAMOUS PRODUCTIONS IN PHOTOGRAPHS, edited by Stanley Appelbaum. 148 photographs from Museum of City of New York show 142 plays, 1883-1939. *Peter Pan, The Front Page, Dead End, Our Town,* O'Neill, hundreds of actors and actresses, etc. Full indexes. 154pp. 9½ x 10.   23241-7 Pa. $6.00

DIALOGUES CONCERNING TWO NEW SCIENCES, Galileo Galilei. Encompassing 30 years of experiment and thought, these dialogues deal with geometric demonstrations of fracture of solid bodies, cohesion, leverage, speed of light and sound, pendulums, falling bodies, accelerated motion, etc. 300pp. 5⅜ x 8½.   60099-8 Pa. $4.00

THE GREAT OPERA STARS IN HISTORIC PHOTOGRAPHS, edited by James Camner. 343 portraits from the 1850s to the 1940s: Tamburini, Mario, Caliapin, Jeritza, Melchior, Melba, Patti, Pinza, Schipa, Caruso, Farrar, Steber, Gobbi, and many more—270 performers in all. Index. 199pp. 8⅜ x 11¼.   23575-0 Pa. $7.50

J. S. BACH, Albert Schweitzer. Great full-length study of Bach, life, background to music, music, by foremost modern scholar. Ernest Newman translation. 650 musical examples. Total of 928pp. 5⅜ x 8½. (Available in U.S. only)   21631-4, 21632-2 Pa., Two-vol. set $11.00

COMPLETE PIANO SONATAS, Ludwig van Beethoven. All sonatas in the fine Schenker edition, with fingering, analytical material. One of best modern editions. Total of 615pp. 9 x 12. (Available in U.S. only)
                        23134-8, 23135-6 Pa., Two-vol. set $15.50

KEYBOARD MUSIC, J. S. Bach. Bach-Gesellschaft edition. For harpsichord, piano, other keyboard instruments. English Suites, French Suites, Six Partitas, Goldberg Variations, Two-Part Inventions, Three-Part Sinfonias. 312pp. 8⅛ x 11. (Available in U.S. only)   22360-4 Pa. $6.95

FOUR SYMPHONIES IN FULL SCORE, Franz Schubert. Schubert's four most popular symphonies: No. 4 in C Minor ("Tragic"); No. 5 in B-flat Major; No. 8 in B Minor ("Unfinished"); No. 9 in C Major ("Great"). Breitkopf & Hartel edition. Study score. 261pp. 9⅜ x 12¼.
                                                    23681-1 Pa. $6.50

THE AUTHENTIC GILBERT & SULLIVAN SONGBOOK, W. S. Gilbert, A. S. Sullivan. Largest selection available; 92 songs, uncut, original keys, in piano rendering approved by Sullivan. Favorites and lesser-known fine numbers. Edited with plot synopses by James Spero. 3 illustrations. 399pp. 9 x 12.   23482-7 Pa. $9.95

CATALOGUE OF DOVER BOOKS

THE DEPRESSION YEARS AS PHOTOGRAPHED BY ARTHUR ROTH-STEIN, Arthur Rothstein. First collection devoted entirely to the work of outstanding 1930s photographer: famous dust storm photo, ragged children, unemployed, etc. 120 photographs. Captions. 119pp. 9¼ x 10¾.
23590-4 Pa. $5.00

CAMERA WORK: A PICTORIAL GUIDE, Alfred Stieglitz. All 559 illustrations and plates from the most important periodical in the history of art photography, Camera Work (1903-17). Presented four to a page, reduced in size but still clear, in strict chronological order, with complete captions. Three indexes. Glossary. Bibliography. 176pp. 8⅜ x 11¼.
23591-2 Pa. $6.95

ALVIN LANGDON COBURN, PHOTOGRAPHER, Alvin L. Coburn. Revealing autobiography by one of greatest photographers of 20th century gives insider's version of Photo-Secession, plus comments on his own work. 77 photographs by Coburn. Edited by Helmut and Alison Gernsheim. 160pp. 8⅛ x 11.
23685-4 Pa. $6.00

NEW YORK IN THE FORTIES, Andreas Feininger. 162 brilliant photographs by the well-known photographer, formerly with Life magazine, show commuters, shoppers, Times Square at night, Harlem nightclub, Lower East Side, etc. Introduction and full captions by John von Hartz. 181pp. 9¼ x 10¾.
23585-8 Pa. $6.95

GREAT NEWS PHOTOS AND THE STORIES BEHIND THEM, John Faber. Dramatic volume of 140 great news photos, 1855 through 1976, and revealing stories behind them, with both historical and technical information. Hindenburg disaster, shooting of Oswald, nomination of Jimmy Carter, etc. 160pp. 8¼ x 11.
23667-6 Pa. $5.00

THE ART OF THE CINEMATOGRAPHER, Leonard Maltin. Survey of American cinematography history and anecdotal interviews with 5 masters—Arthur Miller, Hal Mohr, Hal Rosson, Lucien Ballard, and Conrad Hall. Very large selection of behind-the-scenes production photos. 105 photographs. Filmographies. Index. Originally Behind the Camera. 144pp. 8¼ x 11.
23686-2 Pa. $5.00

DESIGNS FOR THE THREE-CORNERED HAT (LE TRICORNE), Pablo Picasso. 32 fabulously rare drawings—including 31 color illustrations of costumes and accessories—for 1919 production of famous ballet. Edited by Parmenia Migel, who has written new introduction. 48pp. 9⅜ x 12¼. (Available in U.S. only)
23709-5 Pa. $5.00

NOTES OF A FILM DIRECTOR, Sergei Eisenstein. Greatest Russian filmmaker explains montage, making of Alexander Nevsky, aesthetics; comments on self, associates, great rivals (Chaplin), similar material. 78 illustrations. 240pp. 5⅜ x 8½.
22392-2 Pa. $4.50

THE ANATOMY OF THE HORSE, George Stubbs. Often considered the great masterpiece of animal anatomy. Full reproduction of 1766 edition, plus prospectus; original text and modernized text. 36 plates. Introduction by Eleanor Garvey. 121pp. 11 x 14¾. 23402-9 Pa. $6.00

BRIDGMAN'S LIFE DRAWING, George B. Bridgman. More than 500 illustrative drawings and text teach you to abstract the body into its major masses, use light and shade, proportion; as well as specific areas of anatomy, of which Bridgman is master. 192pp. 6½ x 9¼. (Available in U.S. only) 22710-3 Pa. $3.50

ART NOUVEAU DESIGNS IN COLOR, Alphonse Mucha, Maurice Verneuil, Georges Auriol. Full-color reproduction of *Combinaisons ornementales* (c. 1900) by Art Nouveau masters. Floral, animal, geometric, interlacings, swashes—borders, frames, spots—all incredibly beautiful. 60 plates, hundreds of designs. 9⅜ x 8-1/16. 22885-1 Pa. $4.00

FULL-COLOR FLORAL DESIGNS IN THE ART NOUVEAU STYLE, E. A. Seguy. 166 motifs, on 40 plates, from *Les fleurs et leurs applications decoratives* (1902): borders, circular designs, repeats, allovers, "spots." All in authentic Art Nouveau colors. 48pp. 9⅜ x 12¼. 23439-8 Pa. $5.00

A DIDEROT PICTORIAL ENCYCLOPEDIA OF TRADES AND INDUSTRY, edited by Charles C. Gillispie. 485 most interesting plates from the great French Encyclopedia of the 18th century show hundreds of working figures, artifacts, process, land and cityscapes; glassmaking, papermaking, metal extraction, construction, weaving, making furniture, clothing, wigs, dozens of other activities. Plates fully explained. 920pp. 9 x 12. 22284-5, 22285-3 Clothbd., Two-vol. set $40.00

HANDBOOK OF EARLY ADVERTISING ART, Clarence P. Hornung. Largest collection of copyright-free early and antique advertising art ever compiled. Over 6,000 illustrations, from Franklin's time to the 1890's for special effects, novelty. Valuable source, almost inexhaustible.
Pictorial Volume. Agriculture, the zodiac, animals, autos, birds, Christmas, fire engines, flowers, trees, musical instruments, ships, games and sports, much more. Arranged by subject matter and use. 237 plates. 288pp. 9 x 12. 20122-8 Clothbd. $14.50

Typographical Volume. Roman and Gothic faces ranging from 10 point to 300 point, "Barnum," German and Old English faces, script, logotypes, scrolls and flourishes, 1115 ornamental initials, 67 complete alphabets, more. 310 plates. 320pp. 9 x 12. 20123-6 Clothbd. $15.00

CALLIGRAPHY (CALLIGRAPHIA LATINA), J. G. Schwandner. High point of 18th-century ornamental calligraphy. Very ornate initials, scrolls, borders, cherubs, birds, lettered examples. 172pp. 9 x 13. 20475-8 Pa. $7.00

THE COMPLETE WOODCUTS OF ALBRECHT DURER, edited by Dr. W. Kurth. 346 in all: "Old Testament," "St. Jerome," "Passion," "Life of Virgin," Apocalypse," many others. Introduction by Campbell Dodgson. 285pp. 8½ x 12¼.   21097-9 Pa. $7.50

DRAWINGS OF ALBRECHT DURER, edited by Heinrich Wolfflin. 81 plates show development from youth to full style. Many favorites; many new. Introduction by Alfred Werner. 96pp. 8⅛ x 11.   22352-3 Pa. $5.00

THE HUMAN FIGURE, Albrecht Dürer. Experiments in various techniques—stereometric, progressive proportional, and others. Also life studies that rank among finest ever done. Complete reprinting of *Dresden Sketchbook*. 170 plates. 355pp. 8⅜ x 11¼.   21042-1 Pa. $7.95

OF THE JUST SHAPING OF LETTERS, Albrecht Dürer. Renaissance artist explains design of Roman majuscules by geometry, also Gothic lower and capitals. Grolier Club edition. 43pp. 7⅞ x 10¾   21306-4 Pa. $3.00

TEN BOOKS ON ARCHITECTURE, Vitruvius. The most important book ever written on architecture. Early Roman aesthetics, technology, classical orders, site selection, all other aspects. Stands behind everything since. Morgan translation. 331pp. 5⅜ x 8½.   20645-9 Pa. $4.50

THE FOUR BOOKS OF ARCHITECTURE, Andrea Palladio. 16th-century classic responsible for Palladian movement and style. Covers classical architectural remains, Renaissance revivals, classical orders, etc. 1738 Ware English edition. Introduction by A. Placzek. 216 plates. 110pp. of text. 9½ x 12¾.   21308-0 Pa. $10.00

HORIZONS, Norman Bel Geddes. Great industrialist stage designer, "father of streamlining," on application of aesthetics to transportation, amusement, architecture, etc. 1932 prophetic account; function, theory, specific projects. 222 illustrations. 312pp. 7⅞ x 10¾.   23514-9 Pa. $6.95

FRANK LLOYD WRIGHT'S FALLINGWATER, Donald Hoffmann. Full, illustrated story of conception and building of Wright's masterwork at Bear Run, Pa. 100 photographs of site, construction, and details of completed structure. 112pp. 9¼ x 10.   23671-4 Pa. $5.50

THE ELEMENTS OF DRAWING, John Ruskin. Timeless classic by great Viltorian; starts with basic ideas, works through more difficult. Many practical exercises. 48 illustrations. Introduction by Lawrence Campbell. 228pp. 5⅜ x 8½.   22730-8 Pa. $3.75

GIST OF ART, John Sloan. Greatest modern American teacher, Art Students League, offers innumerable hints, instructions, guided comments to help you in painting. Not a formal course. 46 illustrations. Introduction by Helen Sloan. 200pp. 5⅜ x 8½.   23435-5 Pa. $4.00

CATALOGUE OF DOVER BOOKS

THE EARLY WORK OF AUBREY BEARDSLEY, Aubrey Beardsley. 157 plates, 2 in color: *Manon Lescaut, Madame Bovary, Morte Darthur, Salome,* other. Introduction by H. Marillier. 182pp. 8⅛ x 11. 21816-3 Pa. $4.50

THE LATER WORK OF AUBREY BEARDSLEY, Aubrey Beardsley. Exotic masterpieces of full maturity: *Venus and Tannhauser, Lysistrata, Rape of the Lock, Volpone,* Savoy material, etc. 174 plates, 2 in color. 186pp. 8⅛ x 11. 21817-1 Pa. $5.95

THOMAS NAST'S CHRISTMAS DRAWINGS, Thomas Nast. Almost all Christmas drawings by creator of image of Santa Claus as we know it, and one of America's foremost illustrators and political cartoonists. 66 illustrations. 3 illustrations in color on covers. 96pp. 8⅜ x 11¼. 23660-9 Pa. $3.50

THE DORÉ ILLUSTRATIONS FOR DANTE'S DIVINE COMEDY, Gustave Doré. All 135 plates from Inferno, Purgatory, Paradise; fantastic tortures, infernal landscapes, celestial wonders. Each plate with appropriate (translated) verses. 141pp. 9 x 12. 23231-X Pa. $4.50

DORÉ'S ILLUSTRATIONS FOR RABELAIS, Gustave Doré. 252 striking illustrations of *Gargantua and Pantagruel* books by foremost 19th-century illustrator. Including 60 plates, 192 delightful smaller illustrations. 153pp. 9 x 12. 23656-0 Pa. $5.00

LONDON: A PILGRIMAGE, Gustave Doré, Blanchard Jerrold. Squalor, riches, misery, beauty of mid-Victorian metropolis; 55 wonderful plates, 125 other illustrations, full social, cultural text by Jerrold. 191pp. of text. 9⅜ x 12¼. 22306-X Pa. $7.00

THE RIME OF THE ANCIENT MARINER, Gustave Doré, S. T. Coleridge. Dore's finest work, 34 plates capture moods, subtleties of poem. Full text. Introduction by Millicent Rose. 77pp. 9¼ x 12. 22305-1 Pa. $3.50

THE DORE BIBLE ILLUSTRATIONS, Gustave Doré. All wonderful, detailed plates: Adam and Eve, Flood, Babylon, Life of Jesus, etc. Brief King James text with each plate. Introduction by Millicent Rose. 241 plates. 241pp. 9 x 12. 23004-X Pa. $6.00

THE COMPLETE ENGRAVINGS, ETCHINGS AND DRYPOINTS OF ALBRECHT DURER. "Knight, Death and Devil"; "Melencolia," and more—all Dürer's known works in all three media, including 6 works formerly attributed to him. 120 plates. 235pp. 8⅜ x 11¼. 22851-7 Pa. $6.50

MECHANICK EXERCISES ON THE WHOLE ART OF PRINTING, Joseph Moxon. First complete book (1683-4) ever written about typography, a compendium of everything known about printing at the latter part of 17th century. Reprint of 2nd (1962) Oxford Univ. Press edition. 74 illustrations. Total of 550pp. 6⅛ x 9¼. 23617-X Pa. $7.95

YUCATAN BEFORE AND AFTER THE CONQUEST, Diego de Landa. First English translation of basic book in Maya studies, the only significant account of Yucatan written in the early post-Conquest era. Translated by distinguished Maya scholar William Gates. Appendices, introduction, 4 maps and over 120 illustrations added by translator. 162pp. 5⅜ x 8½.

23622-6 Pa. $3.00

THE MALAY ARCHIPELAGO, Alfred R. Wallace. Spirited travel account by one of founders of modern biology. Touches on zoology, botany, ethnography, geography, and geology. 62 illustrations, maps. 515pp. 5⅜ x 8½.

20187-2 Pa. $6.95

THE DISCOVERY OF THE TOMB OF TUTANKHAMEN, Howard Carter, A. C. Mace. Accompany Carter in the thrill of discovery, as ruined passage suddenly reveals unique, untouched, fabulously rich tomb. Fascinating account, with 106 illustrations. New introduction by J. M. White. Total of 382pp. 5⅜ x 8½. (Available in U.S. only) 23500-9 Pa. $4.00

THE WORLD'S GREATEST SPEECHES, edited by Lewis Copeland and Lawrence W. Lamm. Vast collection of 278 speeches from Greeks up to present. Powerful and effective models; unique look at history. Revised to 1970. Indices. 842pp. 5⅜ x 8½. 20468-5 Pa. $8.95

THE 100 GREATEST ADVERTISEMENTS, Julian Watkins. The priceless ingredient; His master's voice; 99 44/100% pure; over 100 others. How they were written, their impact, etc. Remarkable record. 130 illustrations. 233pp. 7⅞ x 10 3/5. 20540-1 Pa. $5.95

CRUICKSHANK PRINTS FOR HAND COLORING, George Cruickshank. 18 illustrations, one side of a page, on fine-quality paper suitable for watercolors. Caricatures of people in society (c. 1820) full of trenchant wit. Very large format. 32pp. 11 x 16. 23684-6 Pa. $5.00

THIRTY-TWO COLOR POSTCARDS OF TWENTIETH-CENTURY AMERICAN ART, Whitney Museum of American Art. Reproduced in full color in postcard form are 31 art works and one shot of the museum. Calder, Hopper, Rauschenberg, others. Detachable. 16pp. 8¼ x 11.

23629-3 Pa. $3.00

MUSIC OF THE SPHERES: THE MATERIAL UNIVERSE FROM ATOM TO QUASAR SIMPLY EXPLAINED, Guy Murchie. Planets, stars, geology, atoms, radiation, relativity, quantum theory, light, antimatter, similar topics. 319 figures. 664pp. 5⅜ x 8½.

21809-0, 21810-4 Pa., Two-vol. set $11.00

EINSTEIN'S THEORY OF RELATIVITY, Max Born. Finest semi-technical account; covers Einstein, Lorentz, Minkowski, and others, with much detail, much explanation of ideas and math not readily available elsewhere on this level. For student, non-specialist. 376pp. 5⅜ x 8½.

60769-0 Pa. $4.50

CATALOGUE OF DOVER BOOKS

THE CURVES OF LIFE, Theodore A. Cook. Examination of shells, leaves, horns, human body, art, etc., in "*the* classic reference on how the golden ratio applies to spirals and helices in nature . . . . "—Martin Gardner. 426 illustrations. Total of 512pp. 5⅜ x 8½.   23701-X Pa. $5.95

AN ILLUSTRATED FLORA OF THE NORTHERN UNITED STATES AND CANADA, Nathaniel L. Britton, Addison Brown. Encyclopedic work covers 4666 species, ferns on up. Everything. Full botanical information, illustration for each. This earlier edition is preferred by many to more recent revisions. 1913 edition. Over 4000 illustrations, total of 2087pp. 6⅛ x 9¼.   22642-5, 22643-3, 22644-1 Pa., Three-vol. set $25.50

MANUAL OF THE GRASSES OF THE UNITED STATES, A. S. Hitchcock, U.S. Dept. of Agriculture. The basic study of American grasses, both indigenous and escapes, cultivated and wild. Over 1400 species. Full descriptions, information. Over 1100 maps, illustrations. Total of 1051pp. 5⅜ x 8½.   22717-0, 22718-9 Pa., Two-vol. set $15.00

THE CACTACEAE,, Nathaniel L. Britton, John N. Rose. Exhaustive, definitive. Every cactus in the world. Full botanical descriptions. Thorough statement of nomenclatures, habitat, detailed finding keys. The one book needed by every cactus enthusiast. Over 1275 illustrations. Total of 1080pp. 8 x 10¼.   21191-6, 21192-4 Clothbd., Two-vol. set $35.00

AMERICAN MEDICINAL PLANTS, Charles F. Millspaugh. Full descriptions, 180 plants covered: history; physical description; methods of preparation with all chemical constituents extracted; all claimed curative or adverse effects. 180 full-page plates. Classification table. 804pp. 6½ x 9¼.
23034-1 Pa. $12.95

A MODERN HERBAL, Margaret Grieve. Much the fullest, most exact, most useful compilation of herbal material. Gigantic alphabetical encyclopedia, from aconite to zedoary, gives botanical information, medical properties, folklore, economic uses, and much else. Indispensable to serious reader. 161 illustrations. 888pp. 6½ x 9¼. (Available in U.S. only)
22798-7, 22799-5 Pa., Two-vol. set $13.00

THE HERBAL or GENERAL HISTORY OF PLANTS, John Gerard. The 1633 edition revised and enlarged by Thomas Johnson. Containing almost 2850 plant descriptions and 2705 superb illustrations, Gerard's *Herbal* is a monumental work, the book all modern English herbals are derived from, the one herbal every serious enthusiast should have in its entirety. Original editions are worth perhaps $750. 1678pp. 8½ x 12¼.
23147-X Clothbd. $50.00

MANUAL OF THE TREES OF NORTH AMERICA, Charles S. Sargent. The basic survey of every native tree and tree-like shrub, 717 species in all. Extremely full descriptions, information on habitat, growth, locales, economics, etc. Necessary to every serious tree lover. Over 100 finding keys. 783 illustrations. Total of 986pp. 5⅜ x 8½.
20277-1, 20278-X Pa., Two-vol. set $11.00

"OSCAR" OF THE WALDORF'S COOKBOOK, Oscar Tschirky. Famous American chef reveals 3455 recipes that made Waldorf great; cream of French, German, American cooking, in all categories. Full instructions, easy home use. 1896 edition. 907pp. 6⅝ x 9⅜.   20790-0 Clothbd. $15.00

COOKING WITH BEER, Carole Fahy. Beer has as superb an effect on food as wine, and at fraction of cost. Over 250 recipes for appetizers, soups, main dishes, desserts, breads, etc. Index. 144pp. 5⅜ x 8½. (Available in U.S. only)   23661-7 Pa. $2.50

STEWS AND RAGOUTS, Kay Shaw Nelson. This international cookbook offers wide range of 108 recipes perfect for everyday, special occasions, meals-in-themselves, main dishes. Economical, nutritious, easy-to-prepare: goulash, Irish stew, boeuf bourguignon, etc. Index. 134pp. 5⅜ x 8½.
23662-5 Pa. $2.50

DELICIOUS MAIN COURSE DISHES, Marian Tracy. Main courses are the most important part of any meal. These 200 nutritious, economical recipes from around the world make every meal a delight. "I . . . have found it so useful in my own household,"—*N.Y. Times.* Index. 219pp. 5⅜ x 8½.   23664-1 Pa. $3.00

FIVE ACRES AND INDEPENDENCE, Maurice G. Kains. Great back-to-the-land classic explains basics of self-sufficient farming: economics, plants, crops, animals, orchards, soils, land selection, host of other necessary things. Do not confuse with skimpy faddist literature; Kains was one of America's greatest agriculturalists. 95 illustrations. 397pp. 5⅜ x 8½.
20974-1 Pa.$3.95

A PRACTICAL GUIDE FOR THE BEGINNING FARMER, Herbert Jacobs. Basic, extremely useful first book for anyone thinking about moving to the country and starting a farm. Simpler than Kains, with greater emphasis on country living in general. 246pp. 5⅜ x 8½.
23675-7 Pa. $3.50

PAPERMAKING, Dard Hunter. Definitive book on the subject by the foremost authority in the field. Chapters dealing with every aspect of history of craft in every part of the world. Over 320 illustrations. 2nd, revised and enlarged (1947) edition. 672pp. 5⅜ x 8½.   23619-6 Pa. $7.95

THE ART DECO STYLE, edited by Theodore Menten. Furniture, jewelry, metalwork, ceramics, fabrics, lighting fixtures, interior decors, exteriors, graphics from pure French sources. Best sampling around. Over 400 photographs. 183pp. 8⅜ x 11¼.   22824-X Pa. $6.00

ACKERMANN'S COSTUME PLATES, Rudolph Ackermann. Selection of 96 plates from the *Repository of Arts,* best published source of costume for English fashion during the early 19th century. 12 plates also in color. Captions, glossary and introduction by editor Stella Blum. Total of 120pp. 8⅜ x 11¼.   23690-0 Pa. $4.50

CATALOGUE OF DOVER BOOKS

SECOND PIATIGORSKY CUP, edited by Isaac Kashdan. One of the greatest tournament books ever produced in the English language. All 90 games of the 1966 tournament, annotated by players, most annotated by both players. Features Petrosian, Spassky, Fischer, Larsen, six others. 228pp. 5⅜ x 8½. 23572-6 Pa. $3.50

ENCYCLOPEDIA OF CARD TRICKS, revised and edited by Jean Hugard. How to perform over 600 card tricks, devised by the world's greatest magicians: impromptus, spelling tricks, key cards, using special packs, much, much more. Additional chapter on card technique. 66 illustrations. 402pp. 5⅜ x 8½. (Available in U.S. only) 21252-1 Pa. $4.95

MAGIC: STAGE ILLUSIONS, SPECIAL EFFECTS AND TRICK PHOTOGRAPHY, Albert A. Hopkins, Henry R. Evans. One of the great classics; fullest, most authorative explanation of vanishing lady, levitations, scores of other great stage effects. Also small magic, automata, stunts. 446 illustrations. 556pp. 5⅜ x 8½. 23344-8 Pa. $6.95

THE SECRETS OF HOUDINI, J. C. Cannell. Classic study of Houdini's incredible magic, exposing closely-kept professional secrets and revealing, in general terms, the whole art of stage magic. 67 illustrations. 279pp. 5⅜ x 8½. 22913-0 Pa. $4.00

HOFFMANN'S MODERN MAGIC, Professor Hoffmann. One of the best, and best-known, magicians' manuals of the past century. Hundreds of tricks from card tricks and simple sleight of hand to elaborate illusions involving construction of complicated machinery. 332 illustrations. 563pp. 5⅜ x 8½. 23623-4 Pa. $6.00

MADAME PRUNIER'S FISH COOKERY BOOK, Mme. S. B. Prunier. More than 1000 recipes from world famous Prunier's of Paris and London, specially adapted here for American kitchen. Grilled tournedos with anchovy butter, Lobster a la Bordelaise, Prunier's prized desserts, more. Glossary. 340pp. 5⅜ x 8½. (Available in U.S. only) 22679-4 Pa. $3.00

FRENCH COUNTRY COOKING FOR AMERICANS, Louis Diat. 500 easy-to-make, authentic provincial recipes compiled by former head chef at New York's Fitz-Carlton Hotel: onion soup, lamb stew, potato pie, more. 309pp. 5⅜ x 8½. 23665-X Pa. $3.95

SAUCES, FRENCH AND FAMOUS, Louis Diat. Complete book gives over 200 specific recipes: bechamel, Bordelaise, hollandaise, Cumberland, apricot, etc. Author was one of this century's finest chefs, originator of vichyssoise and many other dishes. Index. 156pp. 5⅜ x 8. 23663-3 Pa. $2.75

TOLL HOUSE TRIED AND TRUE RECIPES, Ruth Graves Wakefield. Authentic recipes from the famous Mass. restaurant: popovers, veal and ham loaf, Toll House baked beans, chocolate cake crumb pudding, much more. Many helpful hints. Nearly 700 recipes. Index. 376pp. 5⅜ x 8½. 23560-2 Pa. $4.50

CATALOGUE OF DOVER BOOKS

AMERICAN ANTIQUE FURNITURE, Edgar G. Miller, Jr. The basic coverage of all American furniture before 1840: chapters per item chronologically cover all types of furniture, with more than 2100 photos. Total of 1106pp. 7⅞ x 10¾.   21599-7, 21600-4 Pa., Two-vol. set $17.90

ILLUSTRATED GUIDE TO SHAKER FURNITURE, Robert Meader. Director, Shaker Museum, Old Chatham, presents up-to-date coverage of all furniture and appurtenances, with much on local styles not available elsewhere. 235 photos. 146pp. 9 x 12.   22819-3 Pa. $6.00

ORIENTAL RUGS, ANTIQUE AND MODERN, Walter A. Hawley. Persia, Turkey, Caucasus, Central Asia, China, other traditions. Best general survey of all aspects: styles and periods, manufacture, uses, symbols and their interpretation, and identification. 96 illustrations, 11 in color. 320pp. 6⅛ x 9¼.   22366-3 Pa. $6.95

CHINESE POTTERY AND PORCELAIN, R. L. Hobson. Detailed descriptions and analyses by former Keeper of the Department of Oriental Antiquities and Ethnography at the British Museum. Covers hundreds of pieces from primitive times to 1915. Still the standard text for most periods. 136 plates, 40 in full color. Total of 750pp. 5⅜ x 8½.
23253-0 Pa. $10.00

THE WARES OF THE MING DYNASTY, R. L. Hobson. Foremost scholar examines and illustrates many varieties of Ming (1368-1644). Famous blue and white, polychrome, lesser-known styles and shapes. 117 illustrations, 9 full color, of outstanding pieces. Total of 263pp. 6⅛ x 9¼. (Available in U.S. only)   23652-8 Pa. $6.00

Prices subject to change without notice.

Available at your book dealer or write for free catalogue to Dept. GI, Dover Publications, Inc., 180 Varick St., N.Y., N.Y. 10014. Dover publishes more than 175 books each year on science, elementary and advanced mathematics, biology, music, art, literary history, social sciences and other areas.